MW01480452

JIGS TO JACOBITES

4000 years of Irish history

told through *40 traditional set dances*

by Dr Orfhlaith Ní Bhriain and Mick McCabe

Published in 2018 by Independent Publishing Network, Dublin.

Printed by Colorman, Dublin.

Copyright © Dr Orfhlaith Ní Bhriain and Michael McCabe, 2018.

ISBN 978-1-78926-286-5

All right reserved. No part of this publication may be reproduced in any form or by any means without the prior permission of the publisher. Every effort has been made to ensure that credits accurately comply with information supplied. The authors accept responsibility for any errors or omissions.

Design by Mick McCabe.

Illustration by Mick McCabe.

Text by Dr Orfhlaith Ní Bhriain and Mick McCabe.

Jigs to Jacobites receives financial assistance from the Arts Council.

Ní BHRIAIN & M^cCABE'S
Collection of TRADITIONAL SET DANCES
for the DISCERNING READER,
Comprising FORTY *of*
the Most Favorite Slow & Sprightly
SET DANCES *in proper* STYLE & TASTE
with MUSICAL NOTATION,
SONGS *and* STORIES
Also a Treatise with
a HISTORY OF OUR NATIVE LAND
told through these FORTY *selected*
MUSICAL DELIGHTS
Additionally ILLUSTRATED
with all due taste and flair.

(A title page in the style of the early Irish music collections)

THANK YOU

Ár mbuíochas ó chroí le gach éinne a chabhraidh linn an leabhar seo a chur i gcló!

We would like to extend a big thank you to all who helped over the course of this book project. A special thank you to our families and friends for your patience, encouragement and constant support.

Thanks to Aedín, Úna, and Mairéad Ní Bhriain and Seán Ó Briain for reading the various drafts that were sent their way and always responding with a refreshing honesty. Thanks to Paul Kerrigan and Niall Coakley for proofreading so thoroughly.

Thanks are due in particular to Francis Ward and Paul Harrigan for doing the transcriptions and for patiently responding to queries about notation software.

Thanks to Simon Roche and Jerry Malone for their typography, layout, illustration and style advice.

Thanks to Seán and Margaret McCabe and the extended McCabe family for their moral support, to Cath Kilgannon for always seeing the sunny side, and to Billy Greenall for sharing so many set dances tunes all those years ago.

Thanks to the staff and students at the Irish World Academy of Music and Dance, especially Dr Sandra Joyce, Dr Aileen Dillane, Dr Mats Melin, Dr Niall Keegan, Dr Eleanor Giraud, and Dr Catherine Foley, for advice and support over the course of this project.

We would like to acknowledge the following people for answering the many questions we asked you:

Julie O'Donnell, Máire Mhic Aogáin, Carmel McKenna, Aoife O'Brien, Seán Warren, Orlaith Leppard, James and Kathleen McLoughlin, Nancy Troy O'Herlihy, Mairín Ní Ruairc Tuathaigh, Seán Ó Briain, Olive Brennan, Michael Fitzpatrick, Phelim Warren, Gráinne Ni Chonchubair, Dr Síle Denvir, Niamh Dunne, Mickey Dunne, Pat and Ann Hall, Dr Mairéad Ní Bhriain, Dr Francis Ward, Jean Downey and Darach Sanfey.

Thanks are due to Pamela Cotter and the Blas International Summer School of Irish Traditional Music and Dance for expediting the project by inviting us to give the Francis Roche Memorial lecture.

Sincere thanks to Dr John Cullinane for his generosity. He willingly shared his time and expertise and was always available to advise.

A special thanks to Prof. Gearóid Ó Tuathaigh for his constant guidance and sharing of knowledge.

Many thanks to Michael Walsh, Melanie Barber and Richard Arrowsmith for sharing their knowledge of the Morris Dance tradition.

We would like to thank the staff in the following institutions:

The Glucksman Library, University of Limerick, The National Library of Ireland, The Irish Traditional Music Archive and Comhairle Bhéaloideas Éireann.

Thanks to Colin Reid and the team at Colorman printers.

A heartfelt thanks to the Arts Council who had confidence in the project and who provided the funding to enable us to deliver.

Acknowledgements:

The Vanishing Lake was published courtesy of Francis Ward.

The Charlady was published courtesy of Michael Fitzpatrick.

The Wandering Musician was published courtesy of Phelim Warren.

The Blue Eyed Rascal, *The Four Masters* and *The Storyteller* were published courtesy of the O'Doherty and McLaughlin families.

We hope you enjoy *Jigs to Jacobites*

Orfhlaith Ní Bhriain and Mick McCabe
June 2018

FOREWORD

Jigs to Jacobites is a beautifully researched and illustrated collection. It focuses on the set dance, a distinctive dance and tune form in the Irish tradition. This is the first publication dedicated solely to this dance type, a fact which immediately establishes the importance of this text. Forty set dances are presented in a unique and engaging way, with texts, music notations and illustrations; these set dances have been chosen because they are officially recognised by one of the dance organisations central to the transmission and promotion of Irish traditional dance, An Coimisiún le Rincí Gaelacha. The importance of set dances to other organisations such as Comhaltas Ceoltóirí Éireann and An Chomdháil is also recognised.

The Introduction gives details of the targeted audiences, the motivation which led to its production, and its format. Particularly noteworthy are the sections outlining the research process, findings and key concepts – these are invaluable in terms of understanding and navigating the collection. Further contextual information on collectors, composers and dancing masters are given later in the text.

The real joy of this publication lies in the presentation of each individual set dance, detailing the variety of this form. The tunes and dances are brought to life through creative and engaging illustrations, with notations of the tunes, as well as descriptions of the dance steps and song texts (where appropriate). However, in my opinion, it is the accompanying stories that bring life and context to each piece.

These stories touch on many aspects of Irish mythology, history, landscape and occupation, such as the Tuatha Dé Danann, *The Annals of the Four Masters*, foxhunting and roving pedlars. Some of the titles illustrate etymological change (for example, *The Humours of Bandon*), while others show how meaning is contextual (as illustrated in the story accompanying *The White Blanket*). It is fitting that the book features a composition from 2010 – this highlights the vibrancy and continued rejuvenation of this form of dance and music in the present day and into the future.

Dr Orfhlaith Ní Bhriain and Mick McCabe are a formidable pairing. They have shared many music and dance adventures, including as Co-Directors of the Blas International Summer School of Irish Traditional Music and Dance. Dr Ní Bhriain is a valued member of the Irish World Academy of Music and Dance team. She is a researcher with diverse interests and outputs, a performer, a broadcaster and, perhaps most importantly here, she has contributed greatly to Irish dance as musician, dancer, teacher and adjudicator.

Mick McCabe is a renowned flute player, a strong musical voice of the Irish diaspora from Manchester. He is also a talented graphic designer and illustrator, and has creatively led several projects, including the children's book *Is Christmas Cancelled?*. These authors bring a wealth of experience and skill to this text, including a lifetime's engagement with the traditional arts.

This publication will appeal to young and old, and it will have value in a variety of settings. There are several gems waiting to be uncovered by enthusiasts as well as practitioners. It is a unique addition to the increasing volume of texts on Irish traditional dance, song and music, and, importantly, it will be accessible to the community of performers, listeners and observers of these traditions.

Books like these are important. They provide fresh perspectives and insights into repertoires that we sometimes take for granted. I believe that this collection will encourage further research and engagement with the set dance repertoire.

I encourage you to read, play, sing and dance from *Jigs to Jacobites*.

Dr Sandra Joyce
Director
Irish World Academy of Music and Dance
University of Limerick

INTRODUCTION

WHAT? *Jigs to Jacobites* explores 4000 years of Irish history through the lens of 40 traditional set dances. Each set dance title is illustrated. The story of each set dance is told from a general history, music history and dance history perspective. Music notation for each tune is also provided. The website www.trad.dance accompanies this printed book.

WHY? Over the past half-century, Irish music has often become something to listen to rather than dance to, Irish dance has become something to watch and engage with almost as a sport, and Irish song has also tended to become segregated. The recognition of music, song, and dance as a shared Irish cultural expression has lessened. This book illustrates the fact that the historical, social, and performance contexts of Irish music, song, and dance are intrinsically linked. It focuses on set dances as a point of intersection between traditional musician, dancer, and singer, and between past and present.

WHO? This book has several potential audiences…

- General readers who would enjoy an experience of Irish history through the unique lenses of the Irish music, song, and dance traditions.
- Irish dancers, musicians, and singers who would like to learn more about the wider context of their repertoire.
- Dancers who would like to know more about the music they dance to.
- Musicians and singers who would like to know more about the dances associated with each tune or song.
- Students, teachers, and scholars of music, song and dance.

FORMAT

40 SET DANCES The collection of 40 set dances presented in this book is based on the official list of set dances currently permitted at CLRG events. The rationale for this selection is formed primarily from familiarity. Co-author Dr Orfhlaith Ní Bhriain is most familiar with the CLRG dance canon through her roles as a dance teacher and feis musician. Although the selection of set dances included has been correlated with the CLRG official list, information on other dance organisations' inclusion of these set dances has also been added. The authors acknowledge the contributions of all communities to the evolution of Irish music, song and dance.

INDIVIDUAL SET DANCES Each of the 40 set dances included has been allocated its own double-page spread within the book. The lefthand page contains the tune's illustration, and the righthand page contains information on the history of the tune.

ILLUSTRATION For each set dance, an illustration has been created based on the tune's title story (see Tune Title Stories opposite). Many of the illustrations are personal interpretations of people, places or events relevant to the title story as imagined by the illustrator and co-author, Mick McCabe. Other illustrations are based on historical paintings, etchings and illustrations housed in galleries around the world or published in print. For example, *King of the Fairies* is illustrated from imagination, while *Bonaparte's Retreat* is a redrawing of a satirical etching created by Pierre Joseph Moithey in 1815. Despite the variety of sources and inspirations, a common illustration style has been developed to work across all 40 set dances.

HISTORICAL CONTEXT The righthand page has information relevant to the set dance organised under a number of headings.

- **STORY** This details the events, people or places relevant to the tune title.
- **MUSIC** This details the history of the melody of the tune.
- **DANCE** This provides information and anecdotes about the teaching and performance of the set dance.
- **SONG/POEM** Where appropriate, this gives information and verses of a song or poem associated with the set dance.

Each set dance includes staff notation of its melody. Statistics are also provided giving the following details:

- A date relevant to events of significance for the tune (see Music Chronology opposite).
- Time signature of the tune.
- Number of bars in the step.
- Number of bars in the set.

CONTEXTUAL INFORMATION To place the set dances in a wider context, additional information is provided as follows:

- **MAP** This shows locations relevant to the story of each tune title.
- **TIMELINE & TABLE OF CONTENTS** The table of contents provides the chronological timeline that has been followed (see Music Chronology opposite).
- **COLLECTORS** This section details the lives and published works of the major music collectors that contain set dances.
- **COMPOSERS** This section gives information on several composers of set dances.
- **DANCING MASTERS** This section informs on the contributions of a number of key dancing masters.

RESEARCH

PROCESS

Jigs to Jacobites has been co-authored by Dr Orfhlaith Ni Bhriain and Mick McCabe. Both authors are Irish traditional musicians and have a lifetime of experience within the music, song and dance community. In addition to their music, Orfhlaith is a dance educator, TCRG and ADCRG with An Coimisiún le Rincí Gaelacha (CLRG) and Mick is a graphic designer and illustrator. The authors drew on their own experience and expertise throughout this project. The project originated with the simple premise of researching and providing context to traditional set dances. What started with a list of tunes, time signatures and anecdotes has evolved organically into the book as it is presented here. The authors hope that this book will serve as a body of knowledge that other musicians, singers and dancers will be able to reference and add to.

FINDINGS

TUNE TITLE STORIES The titles of tunes in the Irish tradition reflect the socio-economic conditions, the localities, the personalities, the celebrations and commemorations of the times they originated. The titles of the set dances contained in this book are no different. Some of the 40 set dance titles reference clear points in history. Those that do are usually the tunes where the composer is known. For example, *Planxty Hugh O'Donnell* is a known composition of Turlough Carolan. He composed it to commemorate Hugh O'Donnell's marriage to Maud Browne in 1728. For the set dances where the composer is unknown, only an educated guess can be made as to the people, places or events that the titles were first named for. An example of this is *Hurry the Jug*. There is no information about what this title referred to in the mind of its original composer. Instead, the concept of 'passing a jug' has been researched within Irish history. The result is a story recalling the medieval Irish mether tradition.

The authors do not claim that all the stories presented for the set dance are the original title stories. In some instances they are, but in other cases they are merely stories relevant to the theme of the tune title. The nature of each story becomes evident in the reading. The table of contents also gives a brief outline of the rationale for each set dance's designated year.

TITLE ALIASES Equating a story to the title of a tune is further complicated by the nature of music learning within traditional music. In the Irish tradition, tunes are passed between musicians mostly through listening and repeating, rather than through written music notation. Learning is reliant on note pattern recognition skills, more so than tune name recollection.

This reliance on potentially inacurate human memory means that knowledge of the original composer and tune name has been lost in many instances. The composer's name may sometimes be replaced by that of the person teaching the tune. The result is that a single tune may have multiple unrelated titles, and the same title may have multiple unrelated melodies.

MUSIC RESEARCH In this book, tunes with the same names as the 40 set dances have been researched and played to identify which are related, and which are not. Tunes with the same melody as the set dances but with different names have also been researched. Aloys Fleischmann's *Sources of Irish Traditional Music c. 1600-1855*, 1998, has been invaluable for cross-referencing tune names and notation purposes. Likewise, the Port feature of the Irish Traditional Music Archive has proven extremely valuable in allowing access to tune playback facilities.

MUSIC CHRONOLOGY The 40 set dances included in this book have been placed in a chronological order. Each set dance has been designated a year based on themes which appear in its storyline. For example, the melody of the *King of the Fairies* first appears in a Scottish collection from 1786, but the year that has been designated for it within the chronology is 1700 BC. This dating is based on the mythological year that the Tuatha Dé Danann retreated to the Sídhe, henceforth they were known as the fairies. In contrast, the year designated for *Jockey to the Fair* is 1775. This relates to an original publication of the song associated with the set dance melody.

MUSIC NOTATION The music of each of the 40 set dances has been included in staff notation. These provide contours of the melodies as used by Dr Orfhlaith Ní Bhriain during many years of playing at feiseanna (dancing competitions). The notation does not correspond to any particular setting within the music collections but instead represents an interpretation of the set dance tunes. As is normal practice within the tradition, melody playing musicians and dance accompanists may interpret each tune according to personal style. The notation included was transcribed by Paul Harrigan and Dr Francis Ward.

KEY CONCEPTS

There may be certain elements of the Irish music, song and dance tradition which are somewhat less familiar to readers. To ensure maximum accessibility, brief background information and explanation of a number of key concepts is provided here.

MUSIC & SONG

IRISH MUSIC The music played in Ireland as Irish traditional music has a variety of origins. Much of the repertoire is indeed of Irish creation, but much of it also comes from England, Scotland, and further afield. In some instances, we know the composer or songwriter (see Composers, p44-45), but for others, we do not. Regardless of the original origins of a tune or a song, if it has become accepted and played within the Irish music, song and dance community, it is regarded by most as 'now Irish'.

DANCE MUSIC Irish traditional music has a number of different tune types like reels, jigs, hornpipes, set dances, airs and slow airs. Within the song tradition, lyrics in English and Irish have been set to many of these tune types. In addition, many song melodies have been adapted to these tune types. The tunes types and body of music that is appropriate for dancing, is often referred to as 'dance music'.

MUSIC STRUCTURE The vast majority of tunes in the tradition are composed of a series of 8-bar phrases called parts. Most tunes have just two parts, an A and a B (sometimes referred to as first part and second part). Many songs have a similar structure of verse and chorus. A smaller number of tunes have three or more parts.

Most tunes are 'double', meaning that the A part is played twice before moving on to the B part, which is also played twice. This forms an AABB structure. Some tunes are 'single' and follow an AB structure. Regardless of AABB or AB structures, the whole tune is usually played through a number of times before moving on to another tune of the same type, within an arrangement of several tunes.

MUSICAL STYLE The simple musical structure is contrasted by the highly ornate styles of playing and singing that are common within Irish traditional music. Many individuals add intricate ornamentation on and between notes and alter underlying bar phrasing to produce personal phrasing and variation. This personal interpretation can be created in the moment or can be pre-rehearsed for performance or competition.

DANCE

IRISH DANCE Irish dance is an umbrella term referring to a number of dance traditions in Ireland. The Irish dance tradition includes social dances such as set and céilí figure dances, a variety of step dance traditions ranging from improvised sean-nós to traditional step dancing, to competitive step dance, to dancing for shows.

STEP DANCE STYLE The set dance genre is one of the areas within competitive Irish Step dance where individual style and creativity can be showcased. In most instances, the dance teacher composes steps for the set dance allowing for fluidity of movement, musicality, rhythmic complexity, phrasing and ornamentation by the dancer.

Teachers and choreographers will often incorporate motifs which highlight a dancer's strengths. Although the same set dance tune may be used, each teacher will interpret the dance music differently. Additionally, each dancer interprets the music differently when they perform. The fixed steady beat provided by the metronome allows the dancer the freedom to use syncopation and varied phrasing. Dancers accomplish this flow with varying degrees of success. When there is a veritable connection between the dancer and the musician, the entire performance is enhanced.

COMPETITION The first feis was held in 1899 in Macroom, Co. Cork. Dancers danced to live music and were ranked in order by the adjudicators. Today's stages may be much larger and the costumes more flamboyant, but the format of a traditional step dancing competition hasn't changed. Only those who have successfully passed their adjudicators' examination, ADCRG, are permitted to adjudicate at feiseanna organised by CLRG.

ORGANISATIONS A myriad of organisations have shaped the structure and development of the transmission process in competitive Irish Step Dance in the last century. These include but are not limited to An Coimisiún le Rincí Gaelacha (CLRG), Comhaltas Ceoltóirí Éireann (CCÉ), An Chomhdháil, Festival Dance Teachers Association (FDTA), Cumann Rince Naisiúnta (CRN), World Irish Dance Association (WIDA) and the Gaelic Athletic Association (GAA).

SET DANCES

SET DANCE STRUCTURE Set dances are a distinct repertoire within the broader landscape of Irish traditional music and dance. Most set dances do not conform to the usual 8-bar structure associated with Irish traditional music. For a majority, the B part is longer than the A part, but not in a uniform way. Each set dance has its own structure. For example, *The Three Sea Captains* is in 6/8 jig time and has an A of 8 bars, with a B of 20 bars. In contrast, *The Blackbird* is in 2/4 hornpipe time and has an A of 15 bars, followed by a B of 30 bars.

JIG SETS & HORNPIPE SETS Broadly speaking, set dances can be written in jig time 6/8 tempo or in hornpipe rhythm. Tunes written in hornpipe tempo can be notated in 2/4 or 4/4 time.

STEP & SET In musical terms, the normal two-part structure of a tune is divided into A and B, or first part and second part. For set dances alone, dancers refer to the A part as the step and the B part as the set. The step part or lead is danced on both the right and the left legs but the set part is usually only performed on the right and not repeated.

OPEN CHOREOGRAPHY Within the competition setting, all set dance tunes can be danced in an open choreography format. In this format, the teacher works with their dancer to compose new steps and a new choreography unique to that dancer and the set dance tune they have picked.

TRAD SETS A small number of set dances are what are termed 'trad sets' or 'traditional settings'. These are historical steps and choreographies set to specific set dance tunes that are handed down from one generation to the next. In many instances they are the living transmissions of exact steps from the time of the dancing masters to the present. The dancing masters choreographed steps to these set dance tunes to showcase their choreographic skills (see Dancing Masters, p66-67).

DESIGNATED TRAD SETS The number of trad sets in existence is larger than the number allowed in competition. The dance organisations deem certain trad sets to be admissible in competition. There are however traditional settings of other dances such as *The Humours of Bandon* and *The White Blanket* which are not designated as traditional set dances by CLRG. All set dance tunes used for the sets deemed to be traditional may also be interpreted with new choreographies.

SET DANCE TEMPO The minimum tempo for a jig set dance in CLRG is 66 bpm. In general, a jig set would not be danced at a tempo above 74 bmp. The minimum tempo for a hornpipe set dance in CLRG is 76 bpm. Hornpipe sets do not have an upper limit, but are generally not danced at tempi above 112 bpm.

This is not the case for all dance organisations. A feature of the Festival Dance tradition is the extent to which the music can be played at a much lower tempo. This requires the dancer to have excellent balance and poise.

AUTHORS

DR ORFHLAITH NÍ BHRIAIN Dr Orfhlaith Ní Bhriain is an ethnochoreologist and Course Director of the MA in Irish Traditional Dance Performance programme at the Irish World Academy of Music and Dance, University of Limerick, Ireland. Orfhlaith is a registered dance teacher (TCRG), and adjudicator (ADCRG) of Scoil Uí Ruairc (CLRG). As an accomplished performer and teacher of Irish music, song and dance, she delivers workshops and seminars internationally. Orfhlaith is a recognised expert in the Irish traditional music and dance world. She features in many broadcasts and documentaries on radio and television as a cultural commentator.

MICK MCCABE Mick McCabe is a traditional Irish flute player, graphic designer and illustrator. He holds an MA in Irish Traditional Music Performance from the University of Limerick. He has performed as part of numerous groups at festivals including Milwaukee Irish Fest and Lorient Interceltic Festival. Mick has taught tin whistle and flute in many Comhaltas branches and at the Irish World Academy, University of Limerick. Mick was co-director of the Blas International Summer School for Irish Music and Dance with Dr Orfhlaith Ní Bhriain for three years. In recent years Mick's focus has moved from music to a career in design. He works as Lead Designer within education company HMH. He has designed album covers for traditional musicians and illustrated a children's book.

TABLE OF CONTENTS

Date	Page Title	Story	Page
1700 BC	**KING OF THE FAIRIES**	The Tuatha Dé Danann retreat to the Sídhe. Finvara becomes a Fairy King.	1
C. 20 AD	**THE HURLING BOYS**	Setanta plays hurling with King Conor's trainee warrior boys.	3
C. 240 AD	**THE GARDEN OF DAISIES**	The Déise are expelled from Tara and wander around Ireland looking for a home.	5
C. 450 AD	**SAINT PATRICK'S DAY**	Patrick escapes from slavery in Ireland. He later returns to convert the Irish to Christianity.	7
1588	**YOUGHAL HARBOUR**	Sir Walter Raleigh is Mayor of Youghal and plants potatoes on his estate.	9
1589	**HURRY THE JUG**	Whiskey is shared in a mether jug at O'Rourke's Feast.	11
1630	**THE HUMOURS OF BANDON**	The Earl of Cork holds celebrations in Bandon 'under the Sign of the Star'.	13
1636	**THE FOUR MASTERS**	*The Annals of the Four Masters* is completed, documenting Gaelic history for posterity.	15
1640	**THE HUNT**	John Ryan hands over mastership of the Scarteen foxhound pack to his son, Thaddeus.	17
1694	**PLANXTY DAVIS**	Jacobite clans face Williamite forces at The Battle of Killicrankie, Scotland.	19
	COLLECTORS	The lives and published works of the major music collectors that contain set dance tunes.	21
C. 1717	**MISS BROWNE'S FANCY**	Roger Palmer and Mary Browne marry.	23
1724	**PLANXTY DRURY**	John Drury and Elizabeth Goldsmith marry for love on 3rd Mary, 1724.	25
1728	**PLANXTY HUGH O'DONNELL**	Hugh O'Donnell marries Maud Browne.	27
1746	**THE BLACKBIRD**	Bonnie Prince Charlie and the Jacobites face government forces at The Battle of Culloden.	29
1775	**JOCKEY TO THE FAIR**	Jockey proposes to Jenny in love song *Jockey to the Fair*, published in 1775.	31
1782	**RODNEY'S GLORY**	Poet Eoghan Rua Ó Súilleabháin is aboard Rodney's HMH Formidable at The Battle of The Saintes.	33
1783	**THE DRUNKEN GAUGER**	Martha McTier has an unpleasant coach journey with a drunken gauger.	35
1789	**THE RAMBLING RAKE**	Buck Whaley makes it to Jerusalem and back for a wager. He claims his prize money in 1789.	39
1789	**THE DOWNFALL OF PARIS**	Angry crowds storm the Bastille in Paris. The French Revolution begins.	41
1791	**THE ACE AND DEUCE OF PIPERING**	Piper O'Farrell performs on the London stage in *Oscar and Malvina*.	43
	COMPOSERS	The lives and music of several composers of set dance tunes.	45

Date	Page Title	Story	Page
1795	THE PIPER THROUGH THE MEADOW STRAYING	*Piper o'er the meadows straying* is performed in *Zorinski*.	47
1798	THE JOB OF JOURNEYWORK	Journeyman Calico Printer James Smith fights in the 1798 Rebellion.	49
1804	MADAME BONAPARTE	Joséphine is crowned Empress of France, alongside her husband Emperor Napoleon.	51
c. 1807	THE SPRIG OF SHILLELAGH	The 27th Inniskillings adopt *The Sprig of Shillelagh* as their regimental march.	53
1815	BONAPARTE'S RETREAT	Bonaparte is defeated at The Battle of Waterloo and is exiled to Saint Helena.	55
1827	THE THREE SEA CAPTAINS	Britain, France and Russia fight the Ottomans at the naval Battle of Navarino, Greece.	57
1829	THE BLACKTHORN STICK	Stick fighting factions, the Reaskawallahs and the Coffeys hold a peace meeting.	59
c. 1830	THE ROVING PEDLAR	James Duffy, roving pedlar and now publisher, achieves success with Boney's Oraculum.	61
1836	THE ORANGE ROGUE	Orangeman Ogle Gowan forms an alliance with Catholics for his political campaign in Canada.	63
c. 1842	KILKENNY RACES	German travel writer J. G. Kohl observes the racing festival at Kilkenny.	65
	DANCING MASTERS	The lives of key dancing masters who composed set dance steps.	67
1855	RUB THE BAG	*Rub the Bag* is published in *The Petrie Collection of The Ancient Music of Ireland*.	69
1874	THE LODGE ROAD	The Irish Temperance League opens a café kiosk on the Old Lodge Road, Belfast.	71
1898	THE VANISHING LAKE	Colonel John Magee McNeill drowns in Loughareema, Co. Antrim's vanishing lake.	73
1907	IS THE BIG MAN WITHIN?	*Is the Big Man Within* is published in Francis O'Neill's *The Dance Music of Ireland*.	75
c. 1910	THE FIDDLER 'ROUND THE FAIRY TREE	The fairies help Michael Coleman make magical music.	77
1916	THE CHARLADY	Charlady Mrs Caffrey loses her baby daughter to a stray bullet during the 1916 Rising.	79
1935	THE STORYTELLER	Fisherman Conall Ó Beirn tells the story of *The Fairy Piper of Cnoc Áine*.	81
1938	THE WHITE BLANKET	Peggy McTeggart dances *The White Blanket* set dance at the Munster Feis in Cork.	83
1965	THE BLUE EYED RASCAL	*The Blue Eyed Rascal* is published in *A Collection of the Dance Music of Ireland*.	85
1985	THE WANDERING MUSICIAN	Phelim Warren composes *The Wandering Musician* set dance tune for a competition.	87
	REFERENCES		89

SET DANCE STORY LOCATIONS

- **THE VANISHING LAKE** — Loughareema
- **THE BLUE EYED RASCAL** — Derrry
- **THE LODGE ROAD** — Belfast
- **THE STORYTELLER** — Cnoc Áine, Teelin
- **THE FOUR MASTERS** — Drowes
- **THE HURLING BOYS** — Eamhain Macha
- **THE ORANGE ROGUE** — Brockville
- **MISS BROWNE'S FANCY** — Castle Lacken, Killala
- **HURRY THE JUG** — Dromahaire
- **THE FIDDLER 'ROUND THE FAIRY TREE** — Knockgrania
- **PLANXTY DRURY** — Kingsland
- **PLANXTY HUGH O'DONNELL** — Newport
- **SAINT PATRICK'S DAY** — Slane
- **KING OF THE FAIRIES** — Cnoc Meadha, Tuam
- **THE JOB OF JOURNEYWORK** — Prosperous
- **THE CHARLADY & THE DRUNKEN GAUGER** — Dublin
- **THE BLACKTHORN STICK** — Newport
- **RUB THE BAG** — Limerick
- **THE SPRIG OF SHILLELAGH** — Shillelagh
- **KILKENNY RACES** — Kilkenny
- **THE HUNT** — Scarteen
- **THE GARDEN OF DAISIES** — Decies within & without Drum
- **THE WHITE BLANKET & IS THE BIG MAN WITHIN** — Gort na Péiste, Múscraí
- **YOUGHAL HARBOUR** — Youghal
- **THE HUMOURS OF BANDON** — Bandon
- **RODNEY'S GLORY** — Îles des Saintes

- THE BLACKBIRD — Culloden
- PLANXTY DAVIS — Killicrankie
- JOCKEY TO THE FAIR — Dundee
- THE PIPER THROUGH THE MEADOW STRAYING — Cardiff
- THE ACE AND DEUCE OF PIPERING — London
- BONAPARTE'S RETREAT — Waterloo
- THE DOWNFALL OF PARIS & MADAME BONAPARTE — Paris
- THE WANDERING MUSICIAN — Palermo
- THE THREE SEA CAPTAINS — Plyos
- THE RAMBLING RAKE — Jerusalem

KING OF THE FAIRIES

RÍ NA SÍOG

THE AES SÍDHE

1700 BC

HORNPIPE

STORY *Lebor Gabála Érenn* (*The Book of the Taking of Ireland*) contains the ancient origin story of the Irish. It tells that thousands of years ago, six different groups settled in Ireland. The first group was lead by Cessair, Noah's granddaughter. Then came the People of Partholón, the People of Nemed and then the Fir Bolg. The fifth was the Tuatha Dé Danann, the People of the Goddess Danu.

In the *Irish Mythological Cycle*, the Tuatha Dé Danann are described as being supernaturally gifted and long-lived. Their rule came to an end when the sixth people to invade, the Milesians (also known as the Gaels), defeated the Tuatha Dé Danann at The Battle of Druim Lighean. After the battle, it was agreed that the island would be partitioned. The Gaels took the land, and the Tuatha Dé Danann took the Sídhe (the mounds of the Otherworld*). They became the Aes Sídhe, the people of the mounds. (See *Fiddler 'Round the Fairy Tree,* p77)

Another important book, *Annála na gCeithre Máistrí* (*The Annals of the Four Masters,* see p15), records that the first reign of a Gaelic High King (Eremon) dates back to 1700 BC. This marks the year of the Tuatha Dé Danann's retreat to the Otherworld. Although the Tuatha Dé Danann were defeated, the Gaels regarded them as divine, and they became the pre-Christian deities of Ireland.

Entrances to the Otherworld were believed to be through specific mounds, caves and lakes. In *Altram Tige Dá Medar* (*The Fosterage of the Houses of Two Methers*), the Otherworld is divided between the nobles of the Tuatha Dé Danann. Finnbarr (Finvara) received the 'bleak-hilled Sidh Meadha'. This is the hill of Knockma, near Tuam, Co. Galway. It has four cairns, one of which is called Carn Ceasra and is said to be the burial place of Cessair, while another is known as Finvara's Castle. Over time, the old mythology morphed into folklore. The Sídhe become 'the fairies', and Finvara became a King of the Fairies.

In music folklore, the *King of the Fairies* set dance is a summoning tune. If played three times in a row during a celebration, it is said that the king will appear. If the king is pleased with the playing, he will join in the craic. If not, he will disrupt the festivities and cause mischief.

MUSIC The *King of the Fairies* is a variant of the Jacobite tune, *Bonny Charlie*. *Bonny Charlie* appears in James Aird's *A selection of Scotch, English, Irish, and Foreign Airs*, Vol. 2, 1786. The Irish variant of the tune has a related but different second part to the Jacobite versions. The Irish version appears untitled in George Petrie's *The Complete Collection of Irish Music*, 1902. It first appears as *King of the Fairies* in O'Neill's *The Dance Music of Ireland*, 1907.

DANCE The *King of the Fairies* has a traditional dance setting with steps composed by Cormac O'Keeffe from Co. Cork. O'Keeffe was an Irish dance teacher at the Cork Pipers' Club in the early 1900s (see Dancing Masters, p67). He danced the *King of the Fairies* alongside his pupils Nancy and Peggy McTeggart at a performance in the Cork Opera House in 1938. Another versions of *King of the Fairies* also existed. Limerick teacher Kathleen Le Gear noted that Joe Halpin of Limerick had an earlier version. In competitions run by An Coimisiún Le Rincí Gaelacha (CLRG), *King of the Fairies* may be danced as a traditional set, or with newly choreographed steps depending on the tempo of the music.

2/4 time signature

8 bars in step

16 bars in set

* The Otherworld
Also known as Tír na nÓg (The Land of Youth). According to legend, the Otherworld is a supernatural realm outside of time. It is a parallel universe, side by side with ours. It is inhabited by the Celtic deities and the Aes Sídhe who can come and go between both worlds.

TRAD SET

King of the Fairies — Trad

KING OF THE FAIRIES

THE HURLING BOYS
NA BUACHAILLÍ BÁIRE

TALES FROM THE TÁIN

STORY Hurling* is an ancient field game mentioned throughout Irish mythology. It may have been played between the troops of the Tuatha Dé Danann and the Fir Bolg at The Battle of Moytura. For this set dance however, our interest lies in a different story, that of the *Táin Bó Cúailnge (The Cattle Raid of Cooley)*. *The Táin* records our earliest references to boys playing hurling.

In this story, King Conor of Ulster was invited to a banquet being hosted by a smith called Culain. Before he left for the banquet, he visited his young warriors' training-grounds to say goodbye. As usual, the boys were playing a game of hurling, but what he saw that day was no ordinary game. Setanta, the king's nephew, was facing a goal defended by one hundred and fifty boys. He still managed to score. Even when they switched sides, leaving Setanta as the lone goalie against the horde, he defended the goal every time.

Mightily impressed, the king invited Setanta to join his men for the trip to the banquet. Setanta asked if he could finish the game first and follow on later. This was agreed.

THE DEEDS OF CÚ CHULAINN

c. **20** BC

When King Conor was settled in Culain's house, Culain asked the king if anyone else was expected. The king forgot about Setanta and said no, so Culain released his guard-hound to protect the house while King Conor dined.

When Setanta arrived late, the hound attacked him. He used his hurley and shot a ball down the hound's throat, killing it on the spot. Culain was so upset at the death of his guard-hound that Setanta offered to be his guard until a new hound was raised. Henceforth, Setanta was known as Cú Chulainn, Culann's Hound.

Cú Chulainn went on to become a warrior of high renown and was a main character in *The Cattle Raid of Cooley*. This mythological epic centres around queen Medb of Connacht's bid to steal the prize bull of Ulster. When a curse gave child-birth pains to all of the men of Ulster, Cú Chulainn, aged seventeen, had to stand alone against the army of Connacht. Quick-witted, he invoked the right to fight in single combat and spent the next several months defeating Medb's men, one by one.

MUSIC *The Hurling Boys* was collected and published by Petrie (Vol. 2, 1902). He noted that the tune was very popular in the King's County (Co. Offaly). The tune was also known outside of Ireland and was in the repertoire of Suffolk fiddler Fred 'Pip' Whiting. He recorded it on *The Earl Soham Slog*, a compilation album of East Suffolk traditional music released in 1978 by Topic Records.

DANCE This set dance is often performed by young dancers. It has a simple jig rhythm making it suitable for dancers who are learning set dances for the first time.

6/8
time signature

8
bars in step

14
bars in set

* *Hurling*

Regarded as the world's fastest field sport. Two teams of 15 play against each other. Hitting the ball over the crossbar of the H-shaped goals scores 1 point. Hitting it under the crossbar scores 3 points.

The Hurling Boys — Trad

THE GARDEN OF DAISIES
GÁIRDÍN NA NÓINÍNÍ

VASSALS, ABDUCTIONS & WANDERINGS

c. 240 AD

STORY The title and melody of this set dance tune have several possible connections to Co. Waterford. The county is known by locals as The Déise. Supporters of the Waterford Gaelic games teams can regularly be heard shouting 'Up the Déise!'. Déise is an Old Irish word for vassals. Vassals were people who held or rented land on condition of allegiance to a chieftain or king. In early Ireland, there were many vassal tribes such as the Déisi Becc or Déisi Tuisceart.

The ancient Déise tribe of Waterford feature in *Tucait innarba na nDessi* (*The Expulsion of the Déise*), a story from the twelfth-century *Lebor na hUidre* (*Book of the Dun Cow*). Anecdotally, *The Garden of Daisies* is referred to as '*Gáirdín na Déise*', so 'daisies' may be a mistranslation of Déise.

In *The Expulsion of the Déise*, Cormac Mac Airt was High King of Ireland between 226–266 AD and reigned from Royal Tara. His son abducted Forach, an important daughter of the local Déise tribe. Forach's uncle led a band of Déise to Tara to rescue her. When challenged, the king's son refused to return her. Forach's uncle was enraged and ran a spear through the king's son, killing him. A chain from his spear hit King Cormac and took out his eye. They managed to escape with Forach, but the king was livid and expelled the Déise tribe.

The Déise were forced to wander as a landless tribe. They settled in Leinster for some time but were eventually driven out by the Uí Bairrche. They settled in Kilkenny but the king of the Osraige burned down their houses and routed them. They moved on to Munster where they formed an alliance with King Óengus of the Eóganachta through the marriage of Eithne, a foster-daughter of the Déise. As part of her dowry, she requested his help to get the Déise a land of their own. They fought with the Osraige and captured part of their lands south of the River Suir. This became the home of the Déise.

In modern-day Co. Waterford, the Drum-Fineen hills form a divide between two baronies that reference the ancient Déise; Decies within Drum, and Decies without Drum. Perhaps these baronies are the 'Garden of Decies'.

MUSIC *The Garden of Daisies* melody bears a striking resemblance to two airs associated with Waterford. The first of these is the song, *Iníon an Phailitínigh* (*The Palatine's Daughter*). *The Garden of Daisies* uses the same melody as *The Palatine's Daughter*. An orchestral version of this was arranged by composer Seoirse Bodley and used as a signature theme tune for the Irish television series, *The Riordans*. It was also recorded as a polka by Julia Clifford from Sliabh Luachra. The second air that resembles *The Garden of Daisies* is the well-known Irish language song, *Sliabh Geal gCua**. This immigrant song was composed by Pádraig Ó Míleadha who was born in The Déise in 1877 and emigrated to Wales in 1903.

DANCE *The Garden of Daisies* can be danced as a traditional set, or as a new dance choreography for competition. The traditional set was composed by Freddie Murray from Sunday's Well in Cork City, in the early-twentieth century. Freddie and his brother were both stonemasons and travelled frequently with their work. They taught Irish dance in the locations they visited. Most of Murray's original material is still performed today. There are several variations of the end of the Murray setting of *The Garden of Daisies*.

4/4
time signature

8
bars in step

16
bars in set

* Sliabh gCua

Sliabh gCua is a district in West Waterford located between Clonmel and Dungarvan. It was a Gaeltacht area where Irish was spoken as a first language until the late-nineteenth century. Social dances, polkas and hornpipes were very popular there.

The Garden of Daisies — Trad

SAINT PATRICK'S DAY
LÁ FHÉILE PÁDRAIG

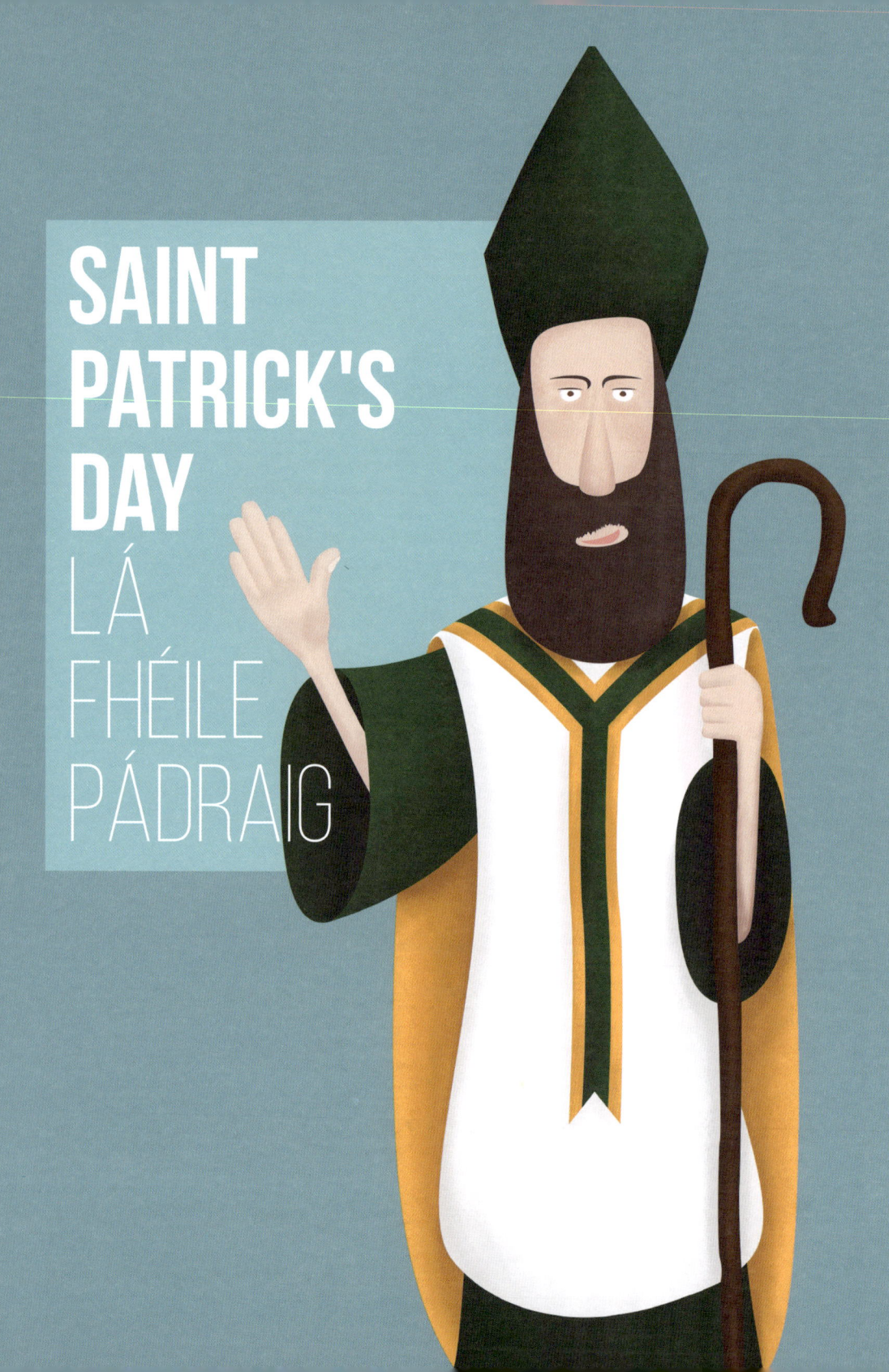

SLAVE TO SAINT

STORY Patrick lived in fifth-century Britain under the declining control of the Roman Empire. His father was a low-level Roman-British noble, and his grandfather was a Catholic priest. Two fifth-century texts, *Epistle to the Soldiers of Coroticus* and the *Confession*, are broadly agreed to be the genuine writing of St. Patrick himself. In these texts, he gives a personal account of his life and his experience of converting the Irish to Christianity.

...I was taken captive when I was about sixteen. I was taken into captivity in Ireland.
Confession, writings of St. Patrick, fifth century.

He was brought to Ireland as a slave and was forced to work as a shepherd in Ulster. The Ireland of that period would have been an alien society to him. It had a well-established system of native laws and customs, and a pagan druidic religion. According to his *Confession*, he escaped from Ireland six years later.

After a second period of captivity, he was reunited with his family. He felt a calling to become a priest. He went for training and returned to Ireland.

...so that I could come to the peoples of Ireland to preach the gospel. (Confession)

In the seventh-century *Life of Saint Patrick* by Muirchú, the story of Patrick was exaggerated to include new legends. These include the lighting of the pascal fire on the Hill of Slane. The familiar story of St. Patrick teaching the holy trinity using a shamrock is more recent, as is the legend that he drove the snakes out of Ireland.

St. Patrick's day, March 17th, is celebrated worldwide and is an enduring expression of Irish culture and identity.

SIGNATURE TUNE & DANCE

c. 450 AD

MUSIC The set dance *Saint Patrick's Day,* also known as *Saint Patrick's Day in the Morning,* has been a popular tune for centuries. Up until the mid 1700s, Irish píob mhór (war pipes) were played when Irish troops went into battle. In *A History of Irish Music*, 1906, historian W. H. Grattan Flood says that *Saint Patrick's Day in the Morning* was played by Irish pipers at The Battle of Fontenoy on May 11th, 1745. This was part of the War of the Austrian Succession and pitched the French and their Irish Brigade against English, Dutch and Austrian forces. After a weary battle, the Irish are said to have won the day for France. This was probably the last appearance of the Irish píob mhór in battle.

Saint Patrick's Day's first appearance in the music collections is within James Oswald's *The Caledonian Pocket Companion*, c. 1750. It was published as part of the musical score for the ballad opera, *Love in a Village*, as performed at the Theatre Royal in London in 1763.

Saint Patrick's Day was the regimental air of La Légion Irlandaise, the Irish Legion within Napoleon's army, which replaced the Irish Brigade that had fought earlier under the French kings.

O'Neill's *Irish Minstrels and Musicians*, 1913, tells an interesting story of Thomas Mahon, an uilleann piper who wanted to play Irish music on an Irish instrument to Queen Victoria when she visited Ireland in 1849. He managed to secure an audience but arrived a day late. The Queen had already left to return to Balmoral in Scotland. He followed them to Balmoral and played *Saint Patrick's Day* for the queen, earning him the title of 'Professor of the Irish Union Bagpipers to Her Most Gracious Majesty, Queen Victoria.'

In America, *Saint Patrick's Day* was published in *Riley's Flute Melodies*, Volume 2, in 1817. The *Saint Patrick's Day* melody has been danced and marched to in North America for some two hundred years. Its popularity has been sustained in part by the large immigrant Irish population who use it as their signature anthem.

Damien Shiels in *The Irish in The American Civil War*, 2013, noted that *Saint Patrick's Day* was played by musicians on both sides of the civil war. The Irish community tended to pledge allegiance to the state where they resided.

Over 150,000 Irish men served in the armies of the North while a further 20,000 fought in the armies of the Southern States. *Saint Patrick's Day* remained popular for many years as a song, country-dance or quickstep. It is played widely today, both at step dance competitions and during parades and festivities on and around March 17th.

DANCE Saint Patrick's Day has a well-known traditional dance setting. It is perhaps the signature step dance of the Irish diaspora, just as the Saint Patrick's Day melody is a signature tune. The historic dance setting is thought to have originated in Limerick. The version most commonly danced today was composed by Stephen Comerford*. The version danced today at CLRG competitions is a shortened version of these older setting. There are other traditional settings composed by Moynihan and Molyneaux (see Dancing Masters, p66). Both the traditional set and newly-composed steps are acceptable in CLRG competition.

6/8 time signature

8 bars in step

14 bars in set

*****Stephen Comerford**
Stephen was a contemporary of the Murray Brothers (early-twentieth century) and one of the dancers associated with the Cork Piper's Club. He composed a number of the steps danced in traditional sets today.

Saint Patrick's Day — Trad

YOUGHAL HARBOUR
CUAN EOCHAILLE

INVASIONS, REBELLIONS & POTATOES

1588

HORNPIPE

STORY Youghal is a town in Co. Cork with a lot of history. In Gaelic Ireland, the local landscape featured a wood of Yew trees, from which it got its name, Eochail. Its strategic location on the south coast of Ireland attracted the attention of Viking raiders. Sigtrygg the Viking established a settlement there in 853.

In 1155 Pope Adrian IV issued a papal bull called *Laudabiliter*. This was a public decree issued to King Henry II of England giving his permission to annex Ireland. The Pope had one condition; that a tax of one penny on every house would go to 'St. Peter' (i.e. the Pope). Thus began the Anglo-Norman conquest of Ireland.

In 1177, Anglo-Norman Robert Fitzgerald took control of the lands of South Munster, including Youghal. By 1350, Youghal was a walled town and an integral part of the Barony of Desmond. Gradually, the Normans in Ireland learned Irish, adopted Irish customs and were largely independent of England. In the mid 1500s friction developed between the Desmonds who wanted to maintain their independence, and Queen Elizabeth I who wanted full English control of Ireland.

The Desmonds rebelled twice but were defeated by English forces. The famous Walter Raleigh took part in the suppression on behalf of the Queen. After the Desmonds were deposed, Raleigh received a knighthood and was granted approximately 40,000 acres of their confiscated land around Youghal.

This is where Youghal becomes a possible place of genesis for one of Ireland's main crops, the potato. Although many historians have disputed it, local legend has it that Sir Walter Raleigh planted a crop of potatoes on his estate after his return from America. This may have been during his tenure as Mayor of Youghal in 1588-1589. An alternative legend claims that the potato was introduced to Ireland when they were washed ashore following the shipwreck of the Spanish Armada off the coast of Co. Clare in the same year, 1588.

MUSIC The melody of *Youghal Harbour*, the set dance, is found in *Francis Roche's Collection of Irish Airs, Marches and Dance Tunes*, Vol. 3, 1927. There are many airs with the title *Youghal Harbour* found in other music collections but these are largely unrelated.

DANCE This is a challenging set dance due to the structure of the *Youghal Harbour* melody. The dancer needs to count five at the end of the introduction before commencing the step (the A part), and between the step and set parts (the B part).

ILLUSTRATION An impressive feature of modern Youghal is the Clock Gate Tower. This was built in 1777 as the town jail and replaced the original Trinity Castle jail. The tower straddles the main street and once acted as the place of public executions.

4/4 time signature

6 bars in step

14 bars in set

Youghal Harbour — Trad

YOUGHAL HARBOUR

HURRY THE JUG

CUIR THART AN CRÚISCÍN

IRELAND'S CEREMONIAL QUAFFING VESSEL

1589

STORY We have no definitive information about what the *Hurry the Jug* title referred to at the time of the tune's composition, but we can infer.

Throughout the ages, Irish celebrations have featured drinking and carousing. If you were at a banquet in medieval Ireland, you might be passed a jug carved from wood. It would have a square mouth, and handles on many sides. This was called a mether, or madder, and it would be filled with wine, whiskey, ale or mead.

The host would pass the mether to the guests, who were expected to take a drink and pass the jug on. It is easy to imagine someone getting impatient and calling out 'hurry the jug!'. The mether is Ireland's ceremonial quaffing vessel.

We can get some idea of the atmosphere at these banquets from the verses of *Pléaráca na Ruarcach*, composed by Hugh MacGauran, and set to music by Turlough Carolan. It commemorates a celebration hosted by the King of Breffni, Brian na Múrtha Ó Ruairc, in 1589.

> *O'Rourke's noble fare – Will ne'er be forgot*
> *By those who were there – Or those who were not.*
> *His revels to keep, – We sup and we dine*
> *On seven score sheep, Fat bullocks and swine*
>
> *Usequebaugh* to our feast – In pails was brought up,*
> *A hundred at least, – And the madder our cup,*
> *O there is the sport! – We rise with the light*
> *In disorderly sort, – From snoring all night.*
>
> Verses 1 & 2 of *Pléaráca na Ruarcach*.

Ó Ruairc was a leading Gaelic lord who ruled lands from Sligo to Cavan. Upon hearing of the Desmond Rebellions, he rose against English encroachment upon his lands. He was executed as a traitor to the English Crown in 1591.

In modern-day Ireland, the mether tradition has largely disappeared from common knowledge. However, the GAA's Liam MacCarthy Cup is modelled on a medieval mether. Although it is made of silver, it is created in the traditional form and is presented annually to the winners of the All-Ireland Senior Hurling Championship.

MUSIC *Hurry the Jug* is a set dance in jig time found in Joyce (1909). It was learned by Joyce as a boy in Co. Limerick in the 1840s. It is also in Roche (Vol. 3, 1927). An alternative setting of the tune is found in *Tunes of the Munster Pipers*, Vol. 1, 1998 by Hugh Shields, one of a series of books that published tunes from the *Goodman Collection* for the first time. The music within *Tunes of the Munster Pipers* was collected by Canon James Goodman in the 1860s. The Goodman version has a similar melody for the A part but a completely different melody for the B part. The version below is modelled on the Joyce melody.

DANCE As well as the solo set dance, *Hurry the Jug* is also the name of a figure dance for eight people. This figure dance was popular in the Limerick area until the 1920s. Maureen Murphy from Abbeyfeale passed on a version of it to Timmy McCarthy in 1994. Timmy 'The Brit' is a set dancing** teacher from London who moved to Co. Cork. The choreography of the *Hurry the Jug* figure dance is an unusual combination of set dancing movements, such as waltz hold gallops, and céilí dance chains and hand movements. It is danced to Slides, a tune type in jig time that is common to the Cork, Kerry and Limerick areas.

6/8 time signature

8 bars in step

16 bars in set

* Usequebaugh
An Anglicised spelling of 'uisce beatha' (water of life), the Irish for whiskey.

** Set Dancing
'Set' here refers to set dancing, an eight-person Irish social dance form derived from French quadrilles. It is a different dance form to solo set dances. Like céilí dances, sets are group figure dances, but they have different steps and movements.

Hurry the Jug — Trad

THE HUMOURS OF BANDON
PLÉARACHA NA BANDAN

BODILY FLUIDS, MOODS & AMUSEMENTS

1630

STORY The meaning of the word humours has changed over the centuries. Up to the middle ages, Islamic and European physicians believed that to be healthy, a balance was needed between the bodily humours. There were four humours, each relating to a different type of bodily fluid. It was believed that imbalances in these fluids could affect physical health and mental temperament. If we were to translate that understanding of the word to our tune title, we might end up with *Bandon Health*.

By the sixteenth century, the idea of mental temperament had taken priority over physical health. Humours during this period came to reflect a person's emotional mood. A translation using this might be *Bandon Vibe*.

Finally, towards the later part of the sixteenth century, humours began to relate to a positive mood, to having fun, and to the comedic. The title translation might now be *Bandon Craic*.

Bandon is a town in Co. Cork. Its first settlement was situated on a natural ford over the River Bandon. This fell within the lands of the Earl of Desmond. After the Earl's unsuccessful rebellions in the late 1500s, the lands of the Desmonds were confiscated by Queen Elizabeth I. The lands around Bandon were redistributed to loyal subjects of the English Crown of Protestant faith.

ILLUSTRATION In the early 1600s, the Earl of Cork bought the lease for the town. When a regional court of law sat in the town in 1630, records of purchases show that the Earl put on a fine inaugural celebration described as being 'under the Sign of the Star'. We can imagine that there was much good humour and merriment in Bandon that night.

One of the legends of the British Royal family is that on the birth of King Charles II in 1630 a noon-day star appeared in the sky. This was seen as highly auspicious. Modern astronomy confirms that Cassiopeia A went supernova at around that time, and would have been visible to the naked eye in the daytime.

MUSIC *The Humours of Bandon* was collected by Goodman c. 1860, and published in Shields (1998). O'Neill (1913) records that *The Humours of Bandon* was still current in nineteenth-century Limerick. A police colleague of O'Neill remembered dancing it in his boyhood to the piping of Newcastle West gentleman musician Jack Moore.

It is likely the tune is much older. George Bennett, in *History of Bandon*, 1862, describes an incident in a church in Kilbrogan, Bandon, in 1690. A Colonel Charles McCarthy raided a church service, along with his troops and three Irish pipers. They are said to have played '*Lille-Burlero*'* and *The Humours of Bandon* in the church, before plundering the town and getting into a shoot-out with the town garrison.

DANCE Maggie Kane, a dancer and teacher from Dublin, learned a version of *The Humours of Bandon* from Kitty Murtagh in 1927. Murtagh later emigrated to America where she continued to teach Irish dancing. There is also a *Humours of Bandon* céilí dance. This is a four-hand jig danced to the tune of *The Humours of Bandon*.

6/8 time signature

8 bars in step

16 bars in set

* Liliburlero

This is an example of a sectarian song which appears at various junctures it the histories of Ireland and England. It is found in Aird (1786) as *Lillie Bulera*, in Petrie (1902) as *Lilibulero* and as *Protestant Boys* in Ryan's *Mammoth Collection* by Elias Howe, 1883. Ironically, it is played as a jig at many feiseanna today.

The Humours of Bandon — Trad

THE FOUR MASTERS
NA CEITHRE MÁISTRÍ

The Age of the World, to this year of the Deluge, 2242. Forty days before the Deluge, Ceasair came to Ireland with fifty girls and three men, Bith, Ladhra and Fintain, their names.
The opening passage of *The Annals of the Four Masters*.

CHRONICLES OF GAELIC HISTORY

1636

HORNPIPE

STORY In 1632, at a Franciscan Abbey near Ballyshannon in Donegal, four scholars began compiling a record of Irish Gaelic history. These are *The Annals of the Four Masters**.

In the decades before, the Gaelic Chieftains had fought The Nine Years War against the English (1593–1603). Led by Hugh O'Neill of Tyrone and Hugh Roe O'Donnell of Donegal, it was a concerted attempt to stop further English incursions upon their lands. The chieftains lost the war to the English, and in 1607 they fled to mainland Europe to seek help from other Catholic powers. They were unsuccessful, and their departure from Ireland became a permanent exile. This was a calamitous event for Ireland as it signalled the end of any serious attempt to stop English colonial rule. The loss of the chieftains is known as The Flight of the Earls and is regarded as a national tragedy.

In the decades that followed, the English began the Plantation of Ulster. This involved a systematic confiscation of the lands of the native Ulster Irish. Subsequently their lands were redistributed to English and Scottish settlers who were loyal to the Crown.

Enter Friar Mícheál Ó Cléirigh of Donegal, a cleric descended from a long line of poets and scholars. When his ancestral lands were lost during the Plantation, he noticed the pressure that Irish society was under and worried that the records of Gaelic Ireland could be lost or destroyed. He gathered archaic books and manuscripts like *The Book of the Taking of Ireland*, and genealogies of important families. He also brought together a group of clerics who were trained in the Gaelic Bardic tradition, and who could understand the archaic form of the Irish language used in the ancient records.

The Annals were painstakingly handwritten in Irish, over several volumes. Taking the early sources, they chronicled a history of Ireland from 2242 BC to 1616 AD. They contain the early Irish creation myths (see *King of the Fairies*, p1), a chronology of the High Kings of Ireland, records of Gaelic tribes and dynasties, of poets and holy men, of wars and plagues, victories and losses. The annals end in 1616, marking the death of Hugh O'Neill in exile.

Completed in 1636, the annals were initially titled *Annála Ríoghachta Éireann (The Annals of the Kingdom of Ireland)*. They later became known as *The Annals of the Four Masters*, in recognition of the scholars who completed them.

MUSIC Along with *The Storyteller* (p81) and *The Blue Eyed Rascal* (p85), the composition of *The Four Masters* set dance is attributed to accordion player and broadcaster, Mr Don O'Doherty. Don and his wife, Ms Mary McLaughlin ADCRG, were leading figures in promoting Irish culture in the North West and beyond. Given his strong connections with Derry and Donegal, it is not surprising that he composed a melody to celebrate the famous *Annals of the Four Masters*.

DANCE Although it is relatively new in that it was composed by Don O'Doherty in the mid-twentieth century (see Composers, p45), *The Four Masters* set dance is now acceptable repertoire for CLRG and An Chomhdháil competitions. It was added to the official list of acceptable dances for CLRG in 2004.

4/4 time signature

8 bars in step

12 bars in set

*** Four Masters**

The Four Masters is an anglicisation of *Na Ceithre Máistrí*, the Four Friars. The Four Masters were:

Mícheál Ó Cléirigh

Cú Choigcríche Ó Cléirigh

Fearfeasa Ó Maoilchonaire

Cú Choigcríche Ó Duibhgeannáin

The Four Masters — Don O'Doherty

THE HUNT
AN FIACH

An maidrín ru', ru', rua, rua, rua,
An maidrín rua 'tá gránna,
An maidrín rua 'na luí sa luachair,
'Gus barr a dhá chluais in airde.

Hark, hark, Finder, Lily agus Piper!
Cruinnigí na gadhair lena chéile
Hark, hark, Truman, is leisce an cú thú
Is maith an cú thú, Bateman!

Tally ho! lena bhonn! Tally ho lena bhonn!
Tally ho! lena bhonn, a choileáinín!
Tally ho! lena bhonn! Tally ho lena bhonn!
Agus barr a dhá chluais in airde!

Verses from *An Maidrín Rua*, a popular Irish language children's song.

The little red fox, roo - roo - roo,
The little red fox that is ugly,
The little red fox lying in the rushes,
And the tips of his ears pricked up.

Hark, hark, Finder, Lily and Piper!
Gather the hounds together
Hark, hark, Truman, you're a lazy dog
Bateman - You're a goodun'!

Tally ho! on his trail! Tally ho on his trail
Tally ho! on his trail, my puppies!
Tally ho! on his trail, Tally ho! on his trail!
And the tips of his ears pricked up.

Translated verses from *An Maidrin Rua*.

CHASING THE FOX

1640

HORNPIPE

STORY The hunting of animals has been a part of Irish life throughout the ages. *The Fenian Cycle* of Irish mythology tells that before *The Expulsion of the Déise* (see *The Garden of Daisies*, p5), Cormac mac Art (226-266 AD) established a band of warriors called the Fianna. The greatest of these was Fionn MacCumhaill, and there are many stories of him and the Fianna hunting wild deer with their hounds. The practice of hunting deer may be gone, but the hunting of foxes is still alive in Ireland.

In an organised hunt, a pack of scent-trained foxhounds track wild foxes under the control of the human 'Master of Hounds' who follows on horseback. The Master uses a hunting horn to let the other horseback followers know where to join the chase. If the hounds catch the scent of a fox, they chase it. If the fox is caught, they may kill it.

In today's Ireland, fox hunting is controversial. Many people want to ban it, while others regard it as a form of necessary pest control. Whatever your viewpoint, fox hunting has a long history.

The most famous Irish hunt is the Scarteen Hunt, in Co. Limerick. This has been run by the Ryan family for over three hundred years. Family records show John Ryan handing over the mastership of a pack of foxhounds to his son, Thaddeus, in 1640. In each generation since, a Ryan has taken up the horn and looked after their pack of Kerry Beagle hounds. The hounds are affectionately called the 'black and tans' after their fur colouring (Note: This use of 'black and tan' predates the nickname of the controversial Royal Irish Constabulary Special Reserve of the 1920s).

The Scarteen Hunt is held in high regard by hunting enthusiasts and attracts riders from all over the world. They are attracted by its unique heritage and also by the farming landscape of Limerick, whose ditches and banks provide a test of skill to any horse rider.

MUSIC *The Hunt* is a set dance in hornpipe time which can be found in *The Petrie Collection of The Ancient Music of Ireland*, 1855. There are two versions of *The Hunt* in O'Neill's *Music of Ireland*, 1903. The second setting, tune 1800, is the version most closely aligned to today's set dance. *The Hunt* is also found in Francis Roche's *Collection of Irish Airs, Marches and Dance Tunes*, Vol. 2, 1912.

DANCE A traditional version of The Hunt was danced by Phil Cahill, a dancing teacher from Co. Kerry, c. 1950. Phil learned his setting from the dancing master Jeremiah Molyneaux, in North Kerry (see Dancing Masters, p66). Phil's student, Irene Gould, was one of the first dance teachers in Co. Kerry to become a registered teacher with CLRG.

4/4 time signature

8 bars in step

12 bars in set

The Hunt — Trad

THE HUNT

PLANXTY DAVIS
PLANCSTAÍ DÁIBHÍS

Illustration
Since the Jacobites were a rebel force, they had no set uniform, except for the blue bonnet. Different accessories were worn on the bonnet to shown rank and clan. The illustration depicts a Jacobean clan chief, whose rank was shown by wearing a feather.

A GAME OF CROWNS, SEASON 1

1694

HORNPIPE

STORY In the late 1600s, King James II of the Scottish House of Stuart was the last Roman Catholic monarch over the Three Kingdoms of England, Scotland and Ireland. His son, James Francis Edward, remained Catholic and was heir to the throne. His daughter, Mary, converted to Protestantism and married the Prince of Orange, William III, from the Dutch Republic.

English Protestant nobles were worried about a Catholic succession and encouraged William of Orange to seize the English throne with James' daughter Mary. In the Glorious Revolution of 1688, King James II of the House of Stuart was deposed. James and his son fled to France and William of Orange was crowned King of England.

James II had a lot of support in Ireland due to his policy of freedom of religion, as well as loyal supporters in England and Scotland. These groups were known as the Jacobites. James sailed to Ireland with French troops and raised a Jacobite army with Irish Catholics. William of Orange sailed to Ireland with English and Dutch troops and raised a Williamite army with Irish Protestants. The two armies lined up against each other on the banks of the Boyne in Co. Meath.

The famous Battle of the Boyne was fought on the 1st July 1690 and was won by William of Orange. After his defeat, King James fled once more to France. This quick retreat angered the Irish, who nicknamed him 'Seamus a' chaca' (James the shit). William's success sealed Protestant rule in Ireland.

This did not end Jacobite resistance though, and many more battles were waged. In Scotland, Bonnie Dundee, the seventh Laird of Claverhouse, rallied the Highland clans loyal to the Jacobite cause. Combined with Jacobites from Ireland, they faced off against William's forces at Killicrankie, Scotland, on the 27th July 1694. This time the Jacobites were victorious, but one-third of their army was killed, including Bonnie Dundee.

MUSIC Today's music and dance community know this tune as *Planxty Davis*, and it appears in O'Neill (1903 & 1907) with that name. *Planxty Davis* evolved from the melody first published as *Irish Gillicranky* in 1694 in the *Atkinson Manuscript*. Grattan Flood (1906) attributes it to Thomas Connellan, who is said to have composed it in honour of The Battle of Killicrankie (see Composers, p44).

DANCE When played as a set dance, *Planxty Davis* is a 16-bar melody written in 2/4 time. In competition, the tune is played through four times in total. This makes it one of the longer set dances. Long set dances are often favoured by teachers and dancers when composing steps and choreography for competition. The long duration gives ample opportunity to showcase the dancer's full range of steps, fitness and stamina. According to John Cullinane* in *Aspects of the History of Irish Dancing*, 1999, *Planxty Davis* was not performed as a competitive set dance prior to 1952.

2/4 time signature

16 bars in step

16 bars in set

*****John Cullinane**

Dr Cullinane is an Irish dance historian from Cork. He qualified as a TCRG in 1965 and later as an adjudicator and examiner with CLRG. His greatest contribution to Irish Dance is his prolific dance publication record. There are over 11 books in the Cullinane collection.

Planxty Davis — Connellan

PLANXTY DAVIS

COLLECTORS

The repertoire played within Irish traditional music consists of many old tunes, plus tunes composed in more recent times with similar style and structure. Many claims have been made as to the antiquity of the older tunes, but dating to any accuracy can be difficult. Tunes attributed as Irish appear in combination collections of English, Scottish, Irish and Welsh music dating from the 1700s. The first collections to publish Irish tunes exclusively date from the 1720s. John and William Neale published *A Collection of the Most Celebrated Irish Tunes* in 1726.

Included here are introductions to several of the prominent Irish music collectors whose publications feature set dances. Edward Bunting, George Petrie, Francis Roche and Patrick W. Joyce all collected their repertoire by notating tunes from traditional musicians and singers. They categorised the notated manuscripts according to tune types like jigs, reels or set dances. These collections of music were published in single volumes or over several volumes.

While concentrating on Bunting, Petrie, Roche and Joyce here, there is a large number of other collectors who have published books over the centuries. The Goodman Collection as published in *The Tunes of the Muster Pipers* series and the collections of Francis O'Neill and Breandan Breathnach were also highly influential Irish music collections.

EDWARD BUNTING
1733-1843

Edward Bunting was one of the first significant music collectors to work in the field of Irish music. Born in Armagh in 1773, he spent much of his life in Belfast. He came from a classical music tradition and was noted as a musical prodigy at a young age. He encountered Irish traditional music at the age of nineteen when he was appointed to notate music played by harpers at the Belfast Harp Festival of 1792.

The Belfast Harp Festival was the first gathering of Irish harpers since the Granard Harp Festival six years previously. It was convened by a group of businessmen, including Henry Joy. The Joy family owned many properties around the city, including a mansion called The Lodge (see *The Lodge Road,* p71). Bunting lived with the Joy McCracken family for more than thirty years.

The purpose of The Belfast Harp Festival was threefold; to revive an interest in harp music, to collect the melodies of harp players, and, to note their style of music for future generations. A total of eleven harpers attended; ten from Ireland and one from Wales. They ranged in age from fifteen to ninety-six. Several of them were blind.

In his role as musical scribe, Bunting notated over forty tunes at the festival. His classical training heavily influenced the style of his transcriptions. This has raised questions surrounding authenticity, but regardless of issues of style, these transcriptions saved tunes that might otherwise have been lost. In addition to his work with the harpers, Bunting also collected melodies from folk musicians from Mayo and other counties on the Western Seaboard. His extensive collection was published in three volumes entitled *Ancient Music of Ireland*, in 1796, 1809 and 1840. Bunting moved to Dublin following his marriage in 1819 and worked as the organist at Saint George's Church. He died in 1843 and is buried in Mount Jerome cemetery.

GEORGE PETRIE
1790-1866

A man of many talents, George Petrie was born in Dublin in 1790 and grew up near Mountjoy Square. He was a talented violinist, artist, antiquarian and archaeologist. Some of his more well-known works of art are displayed in the National Gallery of Ireland.

Petrie worked as head of the Topographical Department for Ordnance Survey Ireland. This allowed him to engage with musicians and singers throughout the country. He was editor of *The Dublin Penny Journal*, a weekly newspaper with articles on Irish history, mythology, geography and culture. He was active in the Royal Irish Academy and was elected to its council in 1829. During his tenure there, he rejuvenated the antiquities committee and oversaw the purchase of many significant Irish manuscripts. He was instrumental in the purchase of an autographed original copy of *The Annals of the Four Masters* (p15).

Petrie collected music for many years, initially as a contributor to the work of other collectors and later for his own publications. For example, he assisted Bunting with his third volume, published in 1840. Petrie remained unconvinced of the reliability of harpers as sources of the music, opting instead for vocalists' interpretations of airs.

He worked with friends such as Eugene O'Curry and John O'Donovan, who were leading contemporary Gaelic scholars. O'Curry transcribed the Irish language lyrics while Petrie collected the melodies and arranged them for piano.

He was a founding member and first President of The Society for Preservation and Publication of Music in Ireland, established in 1851. *Ancient Music of Ireland*, published in 1855, was the first and only such publication by the society. This was Petrie's own collection of music and contained 147 airs with a detailed preface and extensive notes on each melody.

He died in Rathmines in Dublin and was buried in Mount Jerome cemetery. His family entrusted three bound manuscripts of his work to Sir Charles Stanford. Stanford published *The Complete Petrie Collection of Irish Music*, in three volumes, 1902-1905.

PW JOYCE

1827-1914

Patrick Weston Joyce was born in 1827 in the Ballyhoura Hills and raised in Glenosheen, Co. Limerick. His father, Garret, was described as a scholarly shoemaker and his mother was Elizabeth Dwyer. He grew up in an environment steeped with traditional Irish music, song and dance. He was raised in an Irish-speaking district but spoke English as his first language. He learned Irish later through his schooling. His initial education was at a local hedge school. He went on to become a national school teacher, after training at Marlborough Training College, Dublin. He also studied at Trinity College where he completed his third level education.

He was actively involved in many Irish cultural societies including the Royal Irish Academy and the Royal Society of Antiquaries Ireland. He gave many of the tunes he collected to Petrie. Following Petrie's death in 1866, Joyce was concerned that many of his tunes had not been published. He published four music collections himself; *Ancient Irish Music*, 1873, *Irish Music and Song*, 1888-1901, *Irish Peasant Songs*, 1906 and *Old Irish Music and Songs*, 1909.

Joyce also made a considerable contribution to our knowledge of the Irish dance tradition. He was the first to scientifically analyse and classify Irish dance types and identify their salient characteristics. He had been playing for dancers since his childhood and was particularly well suited to this study.

Petrie featured in Joyce's early commentaries on dance. Although Joyce's observations pertained to Munster dancers, Petrie was of the opinion that his classifications could be applied to dance throughout Ireland. Joyce himself referred to dance in the preface to his *Ancient Irish Music*, 1873.

FRANCIS ROCHE

1866-1961

Francis Roche (1866–1961) hailed from the village of Elton in south Co. Limerick. He came from a talented family of musicians and performers and ran an academy of music and dance in Limerick alongside his father and brothers. His father Frank was a dancing master. Young Francis was a violinist, pianist and dancer, and a teacher of music and dance. Their activities were not confined to the traditional arts. They also taught popular classical music and ballroom dancing.

Following in the footsteps of fellow Limerick man P.W. Joyce, Francis began compiling and arranging a collection of music for publication. He was also responding to a demand from students and fellow music teachers.

Being an enthusiastic nationalist and Gaelic League member, he concentrated his focus on Irish traditional tunes. He also included flings and quadrilles, deeming them to emanate from 'related traditions' and considering them Irish by association. Some of the contents of his collection came from his father's manuscripts, other tunes were borrowed from existing written sources, and further tunes were notated directly from the oral tradition.

Roche published his *Collection of Irish Airs, Marches and Dance Tunes* in an initial two volumes in January 1912. The first two volumes quickly sold out and were reprinted. Roche revised both for republication with his third volume in 1927.

MISS BROWNE'S FANCY

ROGHA INÍNE DE BRÚN

A CONFUSION OF SUITORS

JIG

c. 1717

MUSIC Stepping into the world of composition, Miss Browne's Fancy highlights the complicated background of some tunes. This set dance is likely to be either a composition of Turlough Carolan, the famous Irish harper and poet, or of Nathaniel Gow, the famous Scottish fiddle player and composer. (see Composers, p45).

Aloys Fleischmann in *Sources of Irish Traditional Music c. 1600-1855*, 1998, places the first appearance of this melody as published in *Compositions of Carolan* c. 1742. It is listed there as untitled. In *Carolan - The Life Times and Music of an Irish Harper*, 1958, Donal O'Sullivan included the melody of *Miss Browne's Fancy*, also untitled (referring to it as *Tune 180*). It appears in O'Neill (1907) titled as *Planxty Browne*.

To add to the confusion, the same tune appears in *A Third Collection of Strathspey, Reels, etc*, 1792, by Niel Gow, where it is attributed to Nathaniel Gow. There it is named *Miss Margrett Brown's Favourite*. Within Irish dancing circles, the same melody is known as *Miss Brown's Fancy*. Whether Carolan or Gow composed it, there seems to be a consistent connection to a Miss Browne.

STORY If the tune was composed by Carolan, there are several Miss Brownes that the title may refer to:

1. Mary Browne, wife of Theobold Bourke, Sixth Viscount Mayo. (Referred to as Margaret in Grattan Flood, 1906)
2. Maud Browne, wife of Hugh O'Donnell, Newport, Mayo.
3. Mary Browne, wife of Roger Palmer, Castle Lacken, Mayo.

Grattan Flood (1906) wrote that Carolan had an unrequited love for Miss Browne, wife of the Sixth Viscount Mayo. Less is written about Carolan's acquaintance with Maud Browne, but he did compose *Planxty Hugh O'Donnell* in honour of her marriage to Hugh O'Donnell.

Carolan also wrote lovingly of Mary Browne, wife of Roger Palmer, in his eulogy poem *Máire Brún*. Roger Palmer and Mary Browne were married c. 1717. Judging by the sentiments in the poem, she must have suffered a tragic death. *Máire Brún* appears in its original Irish in *Amhráin Chearbhalláin: The Poems of Carolan* by Tomás Ó Máille, 1916.

Sweetness would come to my fingers playing on the cords,
When I think of the fairy-woman of the Browns:
And happiness and gentility would come to all in this world
Who would look askance at the fair-haired one

Close of day, Tuesday, Connacht lost her suavity,
My distress! it is a story of torment,
And the Squire Palmer is henceforth without Máire,
My hat is off to him and I am grieved,

Stanzas 7 & 9 of *Máire Brún*. Translation by Francis Osborn (irishpage.com).

So, Miss Browne's fancy could be Theobold Bourke, Roger Palmer, Hugh O'Donnell, or Turlough Carolan himself!

DANCE Cormac O'Keeffe choreographed a version of *Miss Brown's Fancy* for Nancy Brown Bowler. Born in Cork in 1932, Bowler was taught dance by Kevin O'Connell, Peggy McTeggart, and Cormac O'Keeffe. In 1952, she moved to London and met her husband-to-be, Terry Bowler. They founded the Bowler School of Dancing in 1956. The National Dance Archive of Ireland* holds *The Terry and Nancy Bowler Papers*. This is a collection of correspondence, programmes, press cuttings, and photographs from Terry and Nancy Bowler's dance career.

6/8 time signature

8 bars in step

16 bars in set

*****NDAI**
The National Dance Archive of Ireland (NDAI) is housed at the University of Limerick. It is committed to collecting, preserving, digitising and cataloguing material pertaining to all types of dance in Ireland. It works in partnership with Dance Research Forum Ireland, the Irish World Academy of Music and Dance, and the Arts Council.

Miss Browne's Fancy — Turlough Carolan or Nathaniel Gow

DRURY

& GOLDSMITH

PLANXTY DRURY PLANCSTAÍ DRURY

ADVICE FOR LIFE

1724

STORY   This set dance tune was composed by Turlough Carolan in honour of the marriage of John Drury and Elizabeth Goldsmith, 3rd of May, 1724 (see Composers, p45). The Drury family were one of many families and high society individuals who were patrons of Carolan. He also wrote an accompanying poem to mark this special occasion.

When researching his book on Carolan, Donal O'Sullivan (1958) received a note from a descendant of the Drury line. In the note, Dr Henry C. Drury, M.D. outlined the Drury family genealogy. The Drurys were a high society family of the period. Their family lineage included Sir William Drury, Queen Elizabeth's Lord Deputy of Ireland. John Drury was the eldest son of Edward and Elizabeth Drury of Kingsland, Co. Roscommon.

The Goldsmiths were from more humble origins, but Elizabeth was a cousin of Oliver Goldsmith, a famous Irish poet and novelist.

POEM   There are hints within Carolan's poem that this marriage was outside of the norm. The Drurys were a grand family of the landowner class. It would have been usual for the likes of John Drury to marry someone of similar status. Carolan is obviously pleased to see his patron marrying for love instead of maintaining the status quo.

Welcome to Kingsland, lady with the small fingers and curly hair,
The marriage of this young couple is good news for their friends,
May God Bless John, son of Edward and his sweet wife,
Rich people think there is no pleasure but that of possessing riches,
But I would advise them to act like the good men of old,
and marry for pleasure, not for profit.

Paraphrased translation from *The Complete Carolan Songs & Airs*, Rowsome, 2012.

Unfortunately, the marriage only lasted a year. John died in 1725, aged just 20 years old. John Drury was survived by his only child, Margaret.

MUSIC   The harper Charles Byrne played this tune for Edward Bunting in Belfast in 1792. Bunting noted it down and published it as *Plangstigh Druraidh* in *A General Collection of the Ancient Irish Music*, Vol. 1, in 1796. Edward Light published it around the same time under the name *Planxty Drury* in *A Selection of Scottish and Irish Airs for the Voice*, c. 1795. The famous songwriter Thomas Moore set words to the melody in a song titled *O will you sit in the bow'r with me?*. The song was published in *A Selection of Irish Melodies* in 1807 by John Stevenson. The tune is also known as *Pléaracha Druraí* and *John Drury*.

DANCE   Pupils from the Anna McCoy* School of Irish Dance in Belfast performed a setting of *Planxty Drury* in the 1950s (Cullinane, 1999). The Woodgate sisters also performed Arthur Byrnes' setting of this set dance around this time. Paula Woodgate is a former president of the Canadian Irish Dancing Teachers' Association. Arthur Byrnes of Newry taught céilí dancing at the Gaelic League branch affectionately known as the 'dancing branch', Craobh an Chéitinnigh.

An English country-dance with the title *Jubilee at Eindhoven* is set to the tune of *Planxty Drury*. It can be found in *Belgian Boutades*, by Philippe Callens, 1999.

6/8 time signature

12 bars in step

16 bars in set

*** Anna McCoy**
Born in Belfast in 1925, McCoy danced for Jim Johnson in the 1930s. She took the CLRG teacher's exam aged 18. Her pupils performed in Carnegie Hall, New York, for the Saint Patrick's Day celebrations in the mid 1950s. She was a founding member of An Chomhdháil and also an adjudicator and examiner. (Whelan, 2000)

Planxty Drury — Turlough Carolan

PLANXTY HUGH O'DONNELL

STORY In 1728 Hugh O'Donnell married Maud Browne at Newport, Co. Mayo. Members of the O'Donnell Family were patrons of Turlough Carolan, along with other leading families of that period. Carolan composed *Planxty Hugh O'Donnell* to mark the occasion of their wedding (see Composers, p45).

CLAN The O'Donnell Family lineage stretches back over one thousand six hundred years. In the late fourth century, an ancestor of the O'Donnells is said to have established an effective empire over Ireland, most of Britain and Northern France. He was Niall of the Nine Hostages.

Niall's sons, Conall and Eoghan, left their own mark. Conall conquered the area of modern-day Donegal, while his brother Eoghan conquered the adjoining lands of modern-day Tyrone. Both counties get their Irish names from these ancient princes, Tír Conaill and Tír Eoghain.

St. Patrick is said to have marked Conall's war shield with the sign of the cross. He was told if he followed the sign, his family would have success in battle. It has been part of the family crest ever since.

Eigneachan Ua Domnaill, a descendant of the line of Conall, became the 1st O'Donnell to be King of Tír Conaill (c. 1201).

The Annals of the Four Masters record the 21st O'Donnell, Manus The Magnificent, as a great warrior and poet (see *The Four Masters*, p15).

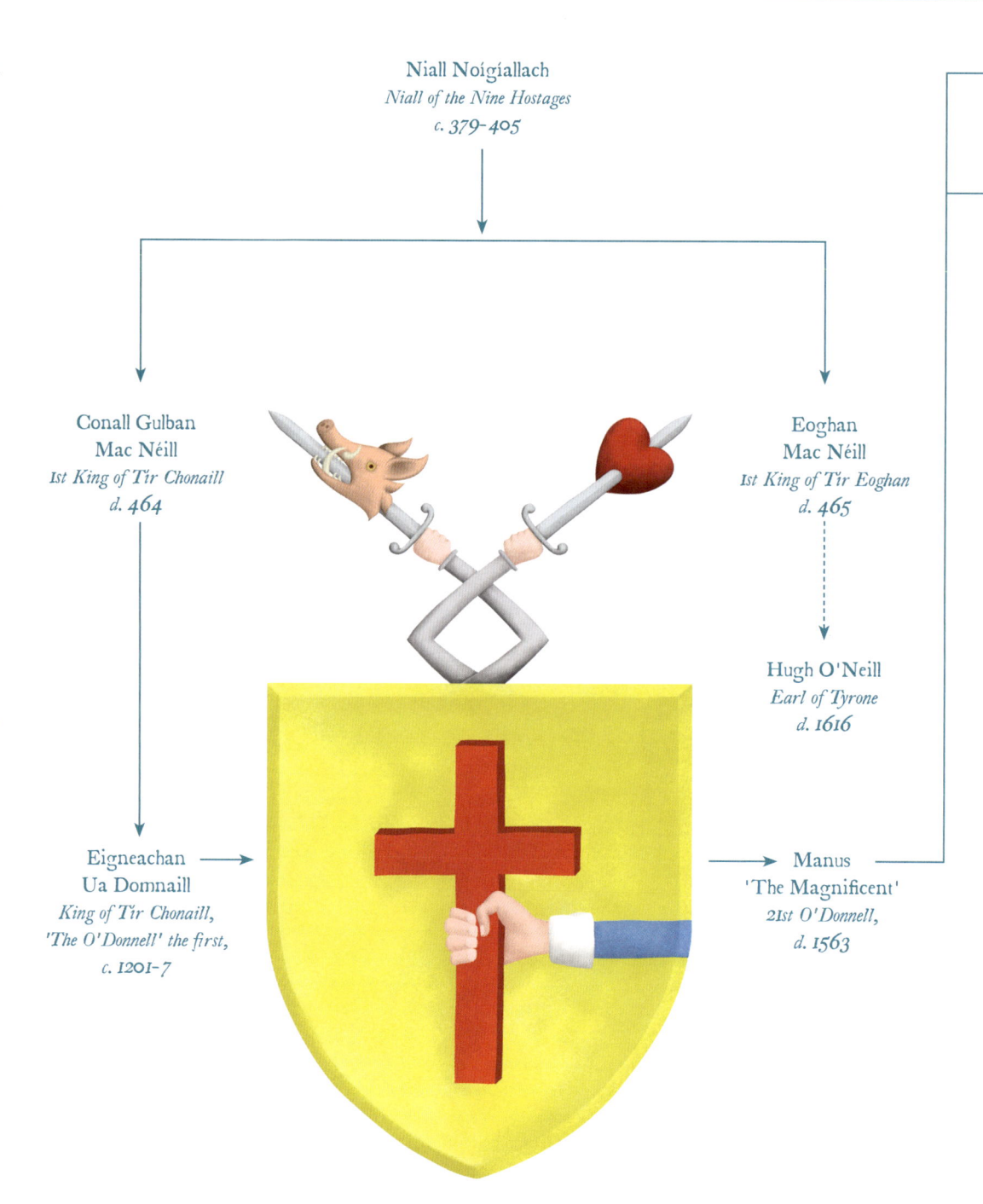

Niall Noígiallach
Niall of the Nine Hostages
c. 379-405

Conall Gulban Mac Néill
1st King of Tír Chonaill
d. 464

Eoghan Mac Néill
1st King of Tír Eoghan
d. 465

Hugh O'Neill
Earl of Tyrone
d. 1616

Eigneachan Ua Domnaill
King of Tír Chonaill, 'The O'Donnell' the first,
c. 1201-7

Manus 'The Magnificent'
21st O'Donnell,
d. 1563

PLANCSTAÍ AODH Ó DÓMHNAILL

JIG

→ **An Calbhach Ó Domhnaill**
22nd O'Donnell
d. 1566

→ **Aodh Mac Maghnusa Ó Domhnaill**
Sir Hugh O'Donnell
23rd O'Donnell
d. 1600

↓

Red Hugh O'Donnell
Aodh Ruadh Ó Domhnaill
24th O'Donnell (confirmed)
d. 1602

Ruairí Ó Domhnaill
25th O'Donnell (confirmed)
Last King of Tír Chonaill
First Earl of Tyrconnell
1592-1602

↓

Hugh O'Neill, the Earl of Tyrone, and Red Hugh led The Nine Years War against English rule in Ireland. The war was lost, and they fled to mainland Europe to raise an army and return. They were unsuccessful and found themselves exiled from Ireland. The continental descendants of this lineage of O'Donnells include an Austrian Count, a member of Napoleon's Council of State, and a Prime Minister of Spain.

→ **Conn O'Donnell**
d. 1583

↓

Sir Niall Garve O'Donnell
25th O'Donnell (disputed)
d. 1625

↓

Col. Magnus O'Donnell
d.1646

↓

Rodger O'Donnell
b. 1630

↓

Col. Manus O'Donnell
d. 1737

↓

Hugh O'Donnell

↓

Hugh O'Donnell, son of Manus O'Donnell, was the subject of Carolan's tune *Planxty Hugh O'Donnell*. Hugh and Maud's son, Neale, was awarded a Baronet of Ireland in 1780 and became Sir Neale. The descendants of this lineage of O'Donnells include Gen. George Blake, a leader of the 1798 Rebellion, and Bram Stoker, the famous author of Dracula.

MUSIC *Planxty Hugh O'Donnell* was composed by Carolan. It was noted down from the playing of harper Charles Byrne in Belfast, 1792, by Edward Bunting. It appears as *Plangsty Hugh O'Donnell* in Bunting (1796). O'Sullivan (1958) published it as *Hugh O'Donnell*. *Planxty Hugh O'Donnell* was recorded in 1978 by Irish dancer and musician Eugene O'Donnell on his album *Slow Airs And Set Dances*, titled *Planxty O'Donnell*.

DANCE *Planxty Hugh O'Donnell* was added to the official list of set dances for CLRG competitions in 2010. It replaced *The Deep Green Pool** set dance. *The Deep Green Pool* was never fully embraced by CLRG musicians due to the unusual repetition of arpeggios. It was rarely danced by competitive dancers. *Planxty Hugh O'Donnell* has since become popular at Oireachtais. Its duration gives dancers an opportunity to showcase their choreography and steps.

1724

6/8
time signature

16
bars in step

16
bars in set

*** Deep Green Pool**
This set dance is still very popular within the Festival Dance tradition.

Planxty Hugh O'Donnell — Turlough Carolan

THE BLACKBIRD
AN LON DUBH

Illustration
Prince Charles Edward Stuart, 1720 - 1788. Eldest son of Prince James Francis Edward Stuart is a painting by William Mosman c. 1750. It depicts Bonnie Prince Charlie wearing the Jacobite blue bonnet with white cockade, plus a blue sash. These Jacobite sysmbols are paired here with the allegorical blackbird.

FOLKLORE The blackbird (an lon dubh) is regarded as a beautiful singer and a good omen. In contrast, other dark birds like the rook, raven or crow have less pleasant bird calls and are regarded as bad omens. We get an idea of the beautiful song of the blackbird from the ninth-century *Blackbird of Belfast Lough...*

Int én bec	*The wee bird*
ro léic feit	*Softly flutes*
do rind guip	*With his peaked bill*
glanbuidi	*Orange gold.*
fo-ceird faid	*Skillfully sounds*
os Loch Laig	*Over Belfast Lough*
lon do craíb	*Bird on the branch*
charnbuidi	*a golden horn.*
Annonymous,	Niall Mac Coitir,
Book of Uí Mhaine.	*Ireland's Birds*, 2015.

STORY In seventeenth-century Ireland, the blackbird assumed a new allegorical role. 1688 saw Catholic King James II of the House of Stuart deposed from the thrones of England and Ireland by William of Orange during the Glorious Revolution. James fled to France with his son, James Francis Edward Stuart. The Irish supported James II as their best hope for religious freedom.

A GAME OF CROWNS, SEASON 2

After his defeat at The Battle of the Boyne (see *Planxty Davis*, p19), and with the Penal Laws*, it was dangerous to talk openly about King James II. In that difficult environment, they used allegory instead. The 'blackbird' came to represent King James II in song and open talk.

Events over the next decades led to James' son, James Francis Edward, attempting an invasion from France to take back the throne. He was unsuccessful, and the last hopes for the House of Stuart fell to his son, Charles Edward Stuart. Charles Edward became popularly known as Bonnie Prince Charlie.

Another invasion attempt was made in 1744, but the fleet got caught in a storm, leaving Charles to raise an army in Scotland. Highland clans, Jacobite troops from Ireland and a small French force rallied to Bonnie Prince Charlie's cause. A number of successful battles were fought until they came face to face with a large government force.

The government army faced off against the Jacobites at The Battle of Culloden, April 16th, 1746. The government forces had a larger army, but a number of bad command decisions lost the day for the Bonnie Prince.

This was the last battle fought on Britsh soil and its result copperfastened English dominance over Britain and Ireland. Charles fled to France after an epic chase across Scotland, commemorated later in *The Skye Boat Song*.

SONG The melody of *The Blackbird* is played both as a set dance and as a slow air. It also has accompanying lyrics that start as follows…

> *On a fair summer's morning of soft recreation,*
> *I heard a fair lady a-making great moan,*
> *With sighing and sobbing and sad lamentation,*
> *A-saying "My Blackbird most royal is flown…"*

First verse from *The Blackbird* as published in Joyce (1909).

According to Joyce (1909) the blackbird in the song's lyrics was an allegory for Bonnie Prince Charlie. Joyce describes the song as being popular throughout Ireland during the early 1800s, and in Limerick and Cork particularly.

MUSIC This set dance appears as *An Londubh (The Blackbird)* in Bunting (1796). Bunting described it as a fine air for the Jacobite lyrics but maintained that 'the air itself bears evident marks of much higher antiquity'. It also appears in Joyce (1909) and Roche (Vol. 2, 1912).

As well as being played in hornpipe time as a set dance, *The Blackbird* is also played without meter as a slow air. This air is in Roche (Vol. 1, 1912). The Irish language song and air *Spailpín a Rúin* is a variant of *The Blackbird* melody. It was recorded as an air by Tommie Potts on his album *Traditional Fiddle Music from Dublin*.

DANCE *The Blackbird* is probably one of the oldest traditional set dances in the dance repertoire. An early setting of it was composed by Keily, a dancing master from Limerick in the early-nineteenth century. Stephen Comerford from Cork also composed a version of the dance in the early 1900s. Joe Halpin from Limerick and Phil Cahill from Kerry also had alternative versions of *The Blackbird*. A new addition to the feis scene is the version composed by Jeremiah Molyneaux from North Kerry. All of these traditional sets are accepted repertoire for competition.

2/4 time signature

15 bars in step

30 bars in set

* **Penal Laws**

The penal laws arose in sixteenth-century England to suppress Catholic power and prosperity, in favour of the new Protestant religion. In Ireland, their effect was extended into the eighteenth century. These laws disenfranchised Catholics in terms of religion, education, property and social activities.

The Blackbird — Trad

JOCKEY TO THE FAIR

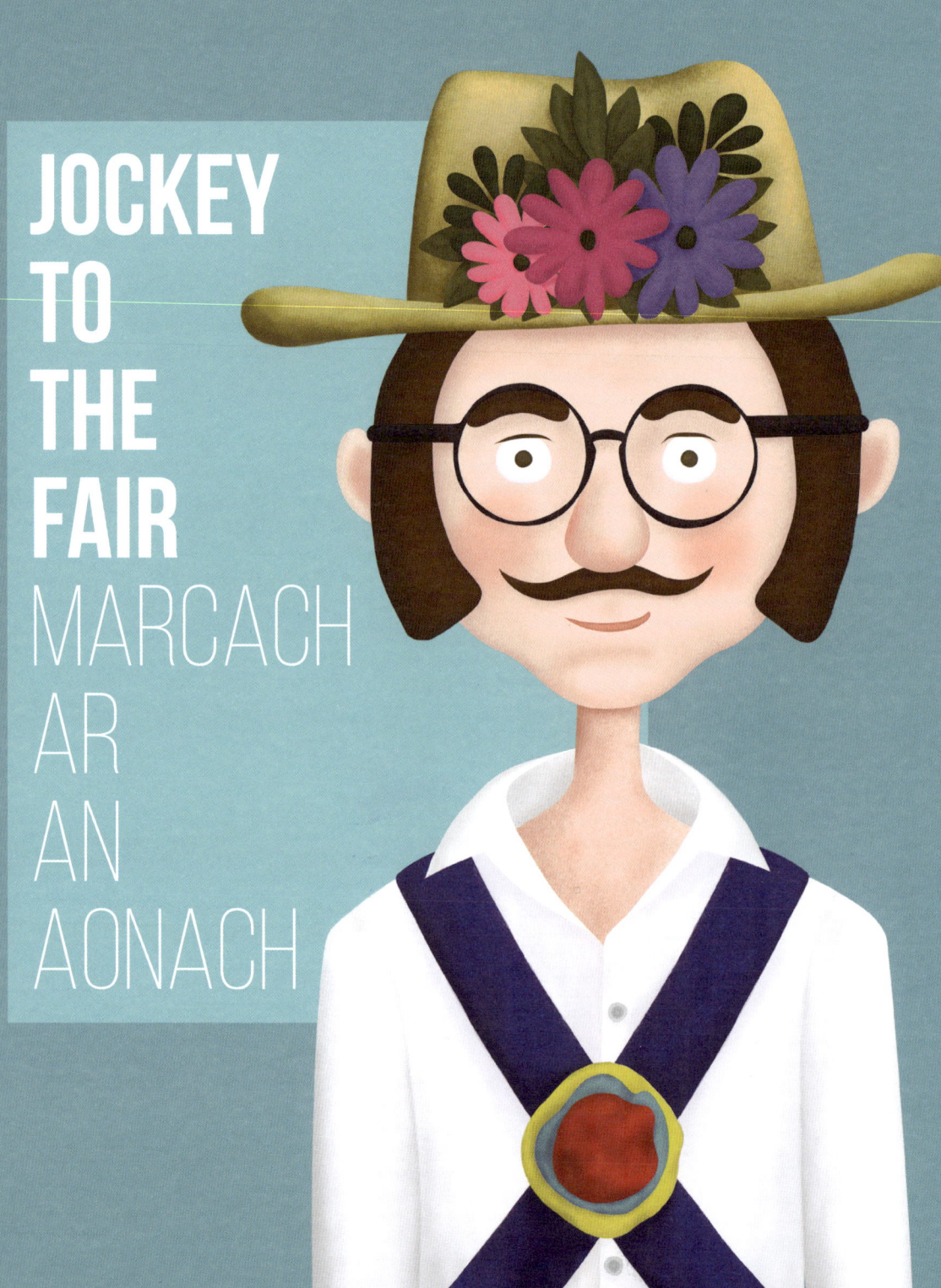

MARCACH AR AN AONACH

'Twas on the morn of sweet May-day,
When Nature painted all things gay;
Taught birds to sing and lambs to play,
And deck'd the meadows fair:
Young Jockey, early in the morn,
Arose and tripp'd it o'er the lawn;
His Sunday coat the youth put on,
For Jenny had vow'd away to run
With Jockey, to the Fair...

Chorus: Repeat the last two lines of each verse

The cheerful parish bells had rung;
With eager steps he trug'd along;
Sweet flow'ry garlands round him hung,
Which shepherds us'd to wear:
He tapp'd the window– "Haste, my dear,"
Jenny, impatient, cried, "Who's there?"
"'Tis I, my love, and no one near;
Step gently down, you've naught to fear "
With Jockey, to the fair.

"My dad and mammy're fast asleep,
My brother's up, and with the sheep;
And will you still your promise keep,
Which I have heard you swear?
And will you ever constant prove?"
"I will, by all the pow'rs above,
And ne'er deceive my charming dove:
Dispel these doubts, and haste, my love,"
With Jockey to the fair.

"Behold the ring," the shepherd cried;
"Will Jenny be my charming bride?
Let Cupid be our happy guide.
And Hymen meet us there!"
The Jockey did his vows renew;
He would be constant, would be true;
His word was pledg'd–away she flew,
With cowslips sparkling with the dew,
With Jockey to the fair.

Soon did they meet a joyful throng,
Their gay companions, blithe and young,
Each joins the dance, each joins the song,
To hail the happy pair.
What two were e'er so fond as they?
All bless the kind, propitious day,
The smiling morn and blooming May,
When lovely Jenny ran away
With Jockey to the fair.

Jockey to the Fair, Chappell (1871).

LOVE, SCOTS & RIGADON

1775

STORY *Jockey to the Fair* is a love song from the Anglo-Scottish broadside* ballads of the seventeenth and early eighteenth centuries. It tells the story of Jockey, a young shepherd, who meets his love, Jenny. It's early in the morning on May Day, and they've made plans to go to the fair. Jenny presses Jockey to see if he'll keep his promise. Jockey produces an engagement ring and asks her to be his bride. Jenny must have accepted, as she goes to the fair with Jockey, meeting their friends on the way.

SONG This song is just one of many 'Jockey' songs. In *The Ballad Literature and Popular Music of the Olden Time* by W. Chappell, 1871, there are seven Jockey songs: *Jockey and Jenny*, *Jockey, away man!*, *Jockey is grown a gentleman*, *Jockey rous'd with love*, *Jockey's escape from Dundee*, *Jockey to the fair*, and *Jockey was a dowdy lad*. The version of *Jockey to the Fair* included in *The Ballad Literature* first appeared in print roughly a hundred years earlier. It was published in *Vocal Music, or The Songster's Companion,* 1775. It was titled using the first line of the song *'Twas on the morn of sweet May-day*.

Chappell describes a sharing of music and song between England and Scotland from the reign of Charles II (1630-1649). Ballads written in the language of lowland Scots were sang to English composed tunes, and English ballads were sung to Scottish airs, creating a shared Anglo-Scottish repertoire. In the mid 1700s, songs with pastoral themes became popular, and Jockey became a stock character within scenes of an idealised Scottish country life.

MUSIC The music notation appears on its own within music collections, starting with *Thompson's Compleat Collection of 200 Favourite Country Dances,* 1770-1785. The tune was still popular in England into the mid 1800s, as it makes a cameo appearance in Thomas Hardy's novel *Far from the Madding Crowd*. *Jockey to the Fair* is the tune that shepherd Gabriel Oak plays on several occasions.

Mark Clark said, "Don't be upset. Times will change. Instead of thinking of the past why don't you play a tune for us?"
Gabriel readily obliged with his favourite tune "Jockey to the Fair".
Far From the Madding Crowd, by Thomas Hardy, 1874.

DANCE *Jockey to the Fair* features in three separate dance traditions; English country dancing, Morris dancing, and Irish step dancing.

Jockey to the Fair was published in Skillern's *Twenty Four Country Dances for the Year 1780*, with dance instructions.

First and second couple pass Rigadon Chasse with partners & Allemand on each side. The same back again & Allmand on each side. First three couples promenade. Cross over one couple and right and left at top.
Jockey to the Fair, Twenty Four Country Dances for the Year 1780.

In the Morris tradition, *Jockey to the Fair* is a corner dance, usually with 6 dancers. Dancers at opposite corners cross to each other's place. The other sides follow, and then the centre dancers. All dance to finish, shouting 'Jockey to the Fair, Oi!'. There are several versions of the corner dance with the *Brackley* version being the most common. There are also two-dancer 'Double Jig' versions such as the *Sherborne*, *Oddington*, and *Ducklington*. These feature more elaborate steps and 'Slows' where the music is slowed down at certain sections. This allows the dancer to perform complicated steps and have more time in the air.

Jockey to the Fair, as a solo step dance, may have been brought to Ireland by the travelling dancing masters. Whatever its origin, it has been adapted and assimilated into the Irish set dance repertoire.

6/8 time signature

8 bars in step

14 bars in set

Broadside
A broadside was a single sheet of paper with poems, ballads or news printed on one side. They were produced cheaply and often sold on the streets by roving pedlars.

Illustration
The inspiration for this illustration is the Jockey Morris Men's Club from Birmingham. They wear all whites, a blue baldrick with a Tudor Rose centrepiece, and straw Panama hats with flowers.

Jockey to the Fair — Trad

RODNEY'S GLORY — GLÓIR RODNEY

Give ear you British Hearts of gold
That do disdain to be controul'd,
Good news to you I will unfold
It is of Brave Rodney's Glory.
Whom always was born with noble hearts
And from his colours never did start,
But boldly takes our Country's part
Against all foes that dare oppose
To blast the bloom of our English Rose,
But now observe my Story —

It was in the year of Eighty two,
The Frenchman knows full well it is true
They thought our fleet for to subdue,
Not far from Old Port Royal.
Full early by the morning light
The prouds of grass appeared in sight
They thought brave Rodney to affright
With colours spread at each mast head
Long pennants flying black white and Red
As a signal for engaging

Our Admiral then gave command
Every man to his quarters stand
All for the sake of Old England,
We will shew them British valour
Then our British Flag display
No tortures could our hearts dismay
Both sides began to cannonade
Their weighty shot we valued not
We played our English pills so hot
We set them in confusion

It's then the French they did combine
To draw their shipping in a line
To sink our fleet was their design
But they were far mistaken
Cannons roar and smoak did rise
Clouds of sulphur filled the skies
That set the grass in great surprise
Brave Rodney's guns and Paddy's sons
Make Keno shake where' er they come
They fear no French nor Spaniards

The Formidable acted well
Commanded by our Admiral
The Old Belfire none could excell,
Our shipping all including
Broadside for broadside we let fly
Where thousands of our men did lie
The seas were of a crimson die
Full deep we stood in human blood
Surrounded by a scarlet flood
We kept such constant firing.

Loud loud cannons they did roar
Which echoed round the Indian shore
Both ship and rigging suffered sore
Not far from Old Port Royal,
Here is a health unto our officers
Seamen bold and jolly tars
That takes delight for to fight
They would sooner for to sink or fight
All for the cause of Old England right
And die for Rodney's glory.

Harding B 25 (1641) c. 1820,
Broadside Ballads Online.

NEW BATTLE TACTICS

1782

STORY George Rodney was a celebrated British naval officer. He started as a volunteer, became a midshipman, and then a lieutenant. He was captain of the HMS Ludlow Castle at the blockade of Scotland around the time of The Battle of Culloden, 1746. He was an Admiral by 1778. Rodney's glory came in April 1782, when he engaged with a French fleet off Îles des Saintes in the West Indies.

The Battle of the Saintes followed the standard line-of-battle naval tactic of the time. The British fleet formed a line, one ship behind another, thirty-six ships long, each ship with up to ninety-eight cannons aboard. Rodney's flagship, HMS Formidable, faced his French counterpart who had formed a line of thirty ships. In standard practice for this naval tactic, the two lines would sail parallel to each other, releasing a barrage of cannon-fire as they passed.

At The Battle of the Saintes, all proceeded as normal, until Rodney saw an opportunity to try to 'break the line'. This innovation had been proposed by John Clerk in his book *An Essay on Naval Tactics*, 1782. A gap between two ships of the French line allowed Rodney to turn the HMS Formidable and sail through. Several more British ships followed Rodney through the gap, dividing the French ships.

The battle was immortalised by Eoghan Rua Ó Súilleabháin, who was serving on the HMS Formidable and experienced it first-hand. Ó Súilleabháin was from Sliabh Luachra in Co. Kerry and was a celebrated poet.

He was well educated and a prolific poet in both Irish and English, but worked as a spailpín, a migrant labourer. He had no love of English rule within Ireland, so when he joined the British Navy, it is doubtful it was by choice. He was a self-confessed womanising rake, and it is likely that he ended up in the navy through compulsory conscription as a result of some indiscretion.

He was present on the HMS Formidable at The Battle of the Saintes and wrote the poem *Rodney's Glory* quickly after the battle. Unusually for Ó Súilleabháin, the poem is full of fawning praise for Rodney and the English cause. The story goes that he was hoping to get on the good side of Rodney in order to secure an honourable discharge from the Navy.

To his chagrin, he was offered a promotion instead. He eventually escaped the Navy by pretending he had an infectious disease. He returned home to Munster to teach.

MUSIC The first publication of this melody with the title *Rodney's Glory* is in Petrie (1905). It is also published in O'Neill (1913) where he recalls hearing his father singing the song *Rodney's Glory*. O'Neill suggests that the air is much older. Fleischmann (1998) adds *Rodney's Glory* as a related tune to Carolan's *Princess Royal*.

DANCE In 1927 Maggie Kane learned a version of *Rodney's Glory* from Denis Cuffe. Cuffe was one of the earliest known Irish dance teachers in Dublin. He learned his solo dancing from the Brewer family and from a dancing master named Horace Wheeler. John Cullinane, in *Aspects of the History of Irish Dancing in Dublin*, 2017, noted that Cuffe may have learned his team dances from Wheeler. Cuffe taught a class in Pearse Street and later at locations in Rathmines and Parnell Square. He was a member of the Irish Dance Teachers Control Board, which met with the Gaelic League* in 1924, in advance of the establishment of An Coimisiún le Rincí Gaelacha.

2/4 time signature

8 bars in step

12 bars in set

*** Gaelic League**
The Gaelic League (Conradh na Gaeilge), was founded in 1893. It sought to establish a canon of Irish dance that would portray a positive image of Ireland. In the 1920s the League set up a Commission of Enquiry to establish guidelines for the conduct of step dance competitions. This resulted in the establishment of CLRG, which still operates under the auspices of the Gaelic League.

Rodney's Glory — Trad

HORNPIPE

RODNEY'S GLORY

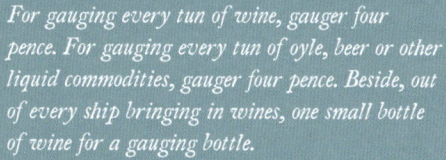

For gauging every tun of wine, gauger four pence. For gauging every tun of oyle, beer or other liquid commodities, gauger four pence. Beside, out of every ship bringing in wines, one small bottle of wine for a gauging bottle.

Statutes Passed in the Parliaments Held in Ireland, 1310 to 1662.

Gauging, from the French word jauge, a "measuring-rod," or "standard," is the art of finding the contents of casks and vessels used by persons under the survey of excise officers, and of fixing and tabulating the same in such manner, that the contents thereof when full, or partly full, may be ascertained by a measuring-rod, or some concise method of computation. The term "Gauger" is sometimes used to epxress the whole business of an excise offficer.

The Excise Officer's Manual and Improved Gauger, 1840.

THE DRUNKEN GAUGER
AN GAUGAER MEISCEACH

PINT MEASURER

1783

STORY The main job of a gauger was to measure and calculate the volume of alcohol inside containers of all shapes and sizes, record the proof level of the alcohol, and collect the taxes due. They had to be clever, as it was no easy task. They had to have a thick skin, as they were not liked. They had to be honest, as the temptation to take a free tipple was great. Many failed on the last requirement.

Mention of drunken gaugers appears in some unlikely places. A threatening letter was found under a Carrick-on-Suir barrack gate in 1824. The anonymous writer was not impressed that the soldiers had confiscated bags of malt from him, under instruction from a drunken gauger.

...I shall, when ye soldiers least expect it, cause the Barrack to be burned, consumed, and levelled to the Ground ... I shall also pull the Tripes out of the drunken Gauger, when I shall meet him.
Captain Rock, Night Errant. The Threatening Letters of Pre-Famine Ireland.

A drunken gauger is mentioned in *Old Murderer*, a short story by Charles Dickens in 1866. Another inebriated gauger can be found in *The Drennan-McTier Letters, 1776-1793*. These letters are a series of personal correspondance between brother and sister William Drennan and Martha McTier, and Martha's huband Sam. In May 1783, Martha wrote to Sam as follows...

I may say without a compliment that the day after I left you was the longest I ever spent. Before one o' clock we were stuffed into a coach where a drunken gauger, a pretty young but not very prim Quaker, and an old gentlewoman had taken possession of the front seats, and a poetical old maid joined us in the back which immediately began to work upon me in the usual manner. The gauger would not give up his seat and I would not accept of the lady's, which being next him I thought worse, as he could not support himself and every whiff of his breath answered the end of hot water.
27 May, postmark. Martha McTier, Dublin, to Sam McTier, Belfast.

William Drennan, Martha's brother, was a member of the Irish Volunteers. These were local militias set up to protect Ireland while British troops were fighting elsewhere. The Volunteers were mostly middle-class Protestants but many had liberal political leanings. Within the Volunteers' ranks, Drennan grew to see the moral need for Catholic Emancipation*. With Wolfe Tone, he was one of the founding members of The Society of United Irishmen. Established in 1791, the United Irishmen aimed to give equal rights to Catholics and establish Ireland as a self-governing republic. To begin with, they tried to enact changes through the political system. They soon realised that little change would come from that route, so they planned a rebellion (see *The Job of Journey Work*, p49, for what happened next).

MUSIC & DANCE Musician Gerald Murphy highlighted a dancing conundrum in *Céim*, the official publication of CLRG, in the early 1980s. There are several strands of confusion surrounding the melody of this set dance. It might be easiest to step through each strand:

1. *The Drunken Gauger* CLRG set dance is an open choreography set dance danced to the tune below.
2. Dancers may ask the competition musicians for *The Funny Tailor* or *The Drunken Gauger*. They will always be played the same melody (see transcription below).
3. In Joyce (1873) this melody is titled *The Funny Tailor*.
4. In Roche (Vol. 3, 1927) the same melody is titled *The Drunken Gauger*.
5. There are several other tunes with *The Drunken Gauger* title that are unrelated to the set dance. These include a slip jig tune in *Joyce's Final Manuscripts*, 1889-1912, and a double jig in Shields (Vol. 1, 1998).

6/8 time signature

15 bars in step

15 bars in set

*** Catholic Emancipation**

The Reformation in Britain established laws to prevent non-Anglicans from holding public office. In Ireland, the Penal Laws restricted the rights of the majority Catholic population. Catholic Emancipation was a campaign to rescind these laws and give equal rights to Catholics. Daniel O'Connell, known as The Liberator, was instrumental in getting the Catholic Emancipation Act passed in Westminster, 1829.

The Funny Tailor (Joyce) / The Drunken Gauger (Roche) — Trad

DRUNKEN GAUGER

PERCUSSIVE ANALYSIS

Oireachtas Rince na Cruinne* 2006, was studied in *An examination of the creative process in competitive Irish step dance,* by Dr Orfhlaith Ní Bhriain, 2010.

All performances by the top five dancers in the ladies and gents 18-19 competition age group were recorded, notated and analysed.

In the ladies section, Kevin Joyce was the musician playing for the set dance round. Thus the melodic transcription is based on his rendition of the tune referred to as *The Drunken Gauger.*

The rhythmic transcriptions reflect the dancers' interpretations of the musical structure. They also demonstrate how their steps can be depicted as rhythmic notation.

Even though three of the dancers danced to the same tune, when we overlay the three percussive lines we can see that their interpretation was quite different.

KEY
- stamp
- en pointe
- silent lift
- click sound

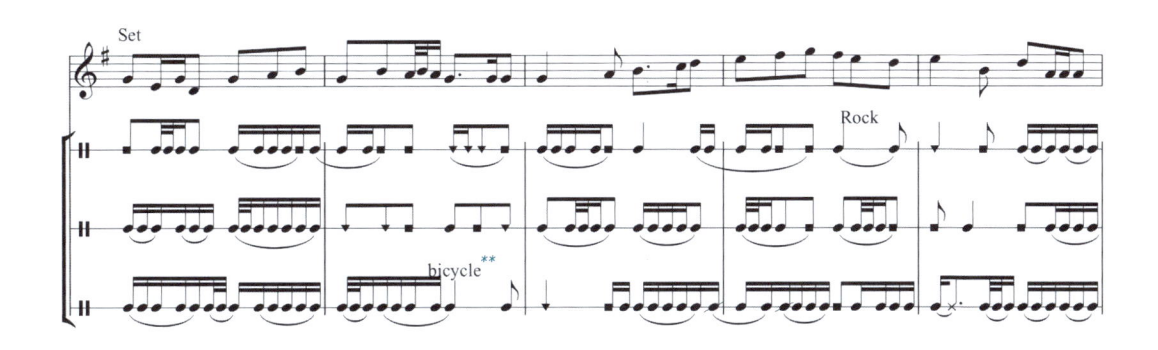

DANCERS' INTERPRETATION

SIOBHAN HACKETT Siobhan Hackett incorporated more toe work and her musical interpretation was quite staccato and contained within the bar lines. Hackett was a pupil of the Aaron Crosbie Academy.

CAOIMHE DOHERTY Caoimhe Doherty used a lot of strong movements such as stamps and drums and repeated motifs for rhythmic effect. Doherty was a pupil of the Doherty Academy.

LEANNE CURRAN Leanne Curran used the same tune setting with a variety of lyrical, musical phrases. She moved between slow and fast movements. Rhythmic patterns were also varied from on-the-beat to more syncopated patterns.

Curran was a pupil of Mona Ní Rodaigh and was the overall winner of her age group at the championships that year.

* The CLRG World Championships in Irish Dance.

** A swift aerial movement which resembles the act of pedalling a bicycle.

THE RAMBLING RAKE

AN RÉICE FÁNACH

JERUSALEM OR BUST

1789

HORNPIPE

STORY In the eighteenth century, exclusive Hellfire Clubs opened across Britain and Ireland. These were places for men in high society to spend their time and fortunes on drinking, whoring, gambling and blaspheming. These philandering aristocrats were called rakes. Rambling low-life gamblers and womanisers were also called rakes*.

The illustration for *The Rambling Rake* is of the infamous eighteenth-century Irish rake, Thomas 'Buck Jerusalem' Whaley. When he was four years old, his father died and left him a fortune. He was educated in a seminary before his mother sent him to France, at the age of sixteen. He had a tutor to take care of him plus a yearly allowance of £900.

He squandered his allowance through gambling and accumulated thousands of pounds of debt. On his return to Dublin, he became a member of the Hellfire Club and gained a reputation for making outlandish bets. His most famous wager was for him to travel to Jerusalem and back within a year, for prize money of £15,000. This would have been a difficult task at the time. He won the wager. His book, *Buck Whaley's Memoirs*, provides a fascinating story of the lands and people he encountered. Here is a condensed version...

Dublin to London. Hired a ship and crew. Sailed from Deal, October 7th, 1788. Storm crossing the Bay of Biscay. Narrowly avoided being boarded by the Moorish Fleet off Cape Spartel. A week in Gibraltar. Explored the caves. Dining. Drinking. Excess. Set sail. Passed by Sardinia, Sicily, and the Greek islands. Reached Smyrna.

Overland to Constantinople. Secured letters of protection to travel through the Ottoman Empire. Spent several weeks touring the city. Fell ill after a hunting trip. Couldn't leave until January 21st. Back to Smyrna. Another storm. Sailed to Acre. Overland to Nazareth. Trouble at Genia. Bribes paid.

February 28th. Jerusalem sighted! Accommodation in Convent. No gambling. Holy Sepulchre and House of Pontious Pilate. Side trip to Bethlehem. Christ's stone manger. Back to Jerusalem. Street of the Cross. March 5th. Certificate from Superior of Convent. Proof!

Left Jerusalem. Attacked by Arabs. Nearly robbed in Napolosa. Escape. Nazareth. Acre. Bought an Arabian horse for small fortune. Set sail. Cyprus. Fun in Nicosi. Tête-à-tête with a lady. Long night. Wine for breakfast. Wild boar hunting. Diner. Sherbet.

Set sail for home. Passed by Crete, Malta and Sardinia. Reached Marseille. Quarantine for 30 days. Paris for 3 weeks. London. Horse envied. Horse poisoned. Dublin! 1789. £15,000 winnings - £8,000 expenses = £7,000 profit. 2 years of play!

MUSIC *The Rambling Rake* appears in O'Neill (1903) and Roche (1927). The melody of the step section (the A part) is quite similar to the tune of *King of the Fairies*. There is a reel of the same title in O'Neill's *Waifs and Strays of Gaelic Melody*, 1922. This bears no similarity to the set dance.

The term rake is found in many Irish tune titles such as *The Rakes of Mallow*, *The Rake's March* and *Rakish Paddy*.

DANCE Unlike many set dances, *The Rambling Rake* has a straightforward tune structure with 8 bars in the step part, and doubled to 16 bars in the set part. Áine Ní Thuathaigh, daughter of Úna Ní Ruairc from Limerick, danced *The Rambling Rake* when she won the All-Ireland Championship in the 1950s. It is thought that the choreography for the set originated with Ita Cadwell, who was later associated with An Chomhdháil and then Cumann Rince Náisiúnta.

4/4 time signature

8 bars in step

16 bars in set

*****Rake**
Short for rake-hell. A term originally used during the seventeenth century to describe members of the 'Merry Gang' of King Charles II of England. This high-society group, including the king himself, were known to be womanisers, heavy drinkers and gamblers.

The Rambling Rake — Trad

THE DOWNFALL OF PARIS
TITIM PHÁRAS

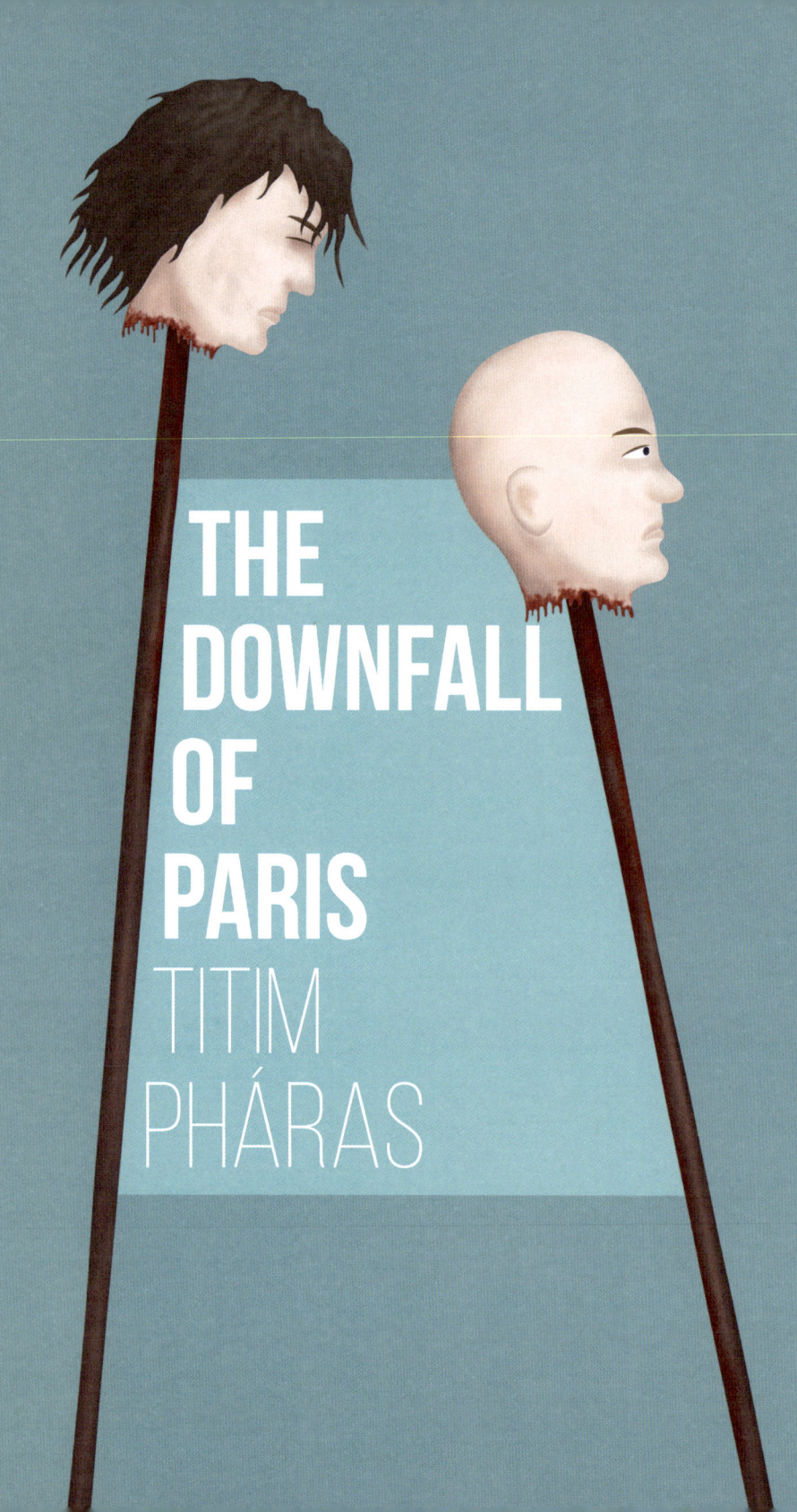

STORY In the late 1700s, French society was in turmoil. The country was in debt due to the king's extravigant way of life. The ruling classes lived in luxury, while the commoners lived in misery. Only commoners paid tax, and with ongoing food shortages, civil unrest was brewing.

The country was organised under a system of three 'Estates' representative of the clergy, the nobility, and the commoners. In 1789, King Louis XVI called a meeting of the Estates. Controversially, he proposed that all three Estates should pay tax. The clergy and nobility didn't want this, and the commoners were tired of paying for it all. The Third Estate, the representatives of the commoners, met separately and declared a National Constituent Assembly. They vowed to create a new constitution and to enact a wide range of reforms.

The king initially resisted the changes and summoned extra troops to Paris. The people rebelled. Militias formed and demands were made to Paris' Mayor de Flesselles, to supply weapons. He gave them inacurate information and they raided the Hôtel des Invalides, finding muskets, but no ammunition. The gunpowder had been moved to the Bastille, a hated prison.

On July 14th, 1789, crowds gathered outside the Bastille demanding its surrender and its gunpowder. Comander of the Bastille, Governor de Launay, refused to meet their demands but entered into negotiations. The crowd grew restless and pushed into the prison's outer courtyard. Shots were fired and the scene turned ugly. This led to what is now known as 'the storming of the Bastille'. With armed support arriving for the crowd, Governor de Launay called a cease-fire. He indicated a willingness to surrender but he was seized by the crowd and stabbed.

Shortly after, an angry mob surrounded Paris City Hall. They accused Mayor de Flesselles of treachery. He was shot dead and beheaded. The jubilant crowd put his head on a pike, along with the severed head of Governor de Launay, and they were paraded around Paris.

Paris had fallen and the French Revolution had begun.

HEADS WILL ROLL

1789

SONG By 1790, reforms had led to a constitutional monarchy and a representative Assembly. This was celebrated with a festival where a new song, Ça Ira, became popular. It had a quick, bright melody and a repetitive, positive chorus of 'ça ira' (it'll be fine).

Ah! ça ira, ça ira, ça ira
Réjouissons nous, le bon temps viendra
Let's rejoice, good times will come.

Stability was short-lived, however, as the king tried to escape the country in 1791. He was caught and tried for treason. In 1793, King Louis XVI was executed by guillotine. This marked the beginning of the Reign of Terror, which saw the execution of over 15,000 'enemies of the Revolution'. The words of Ça Ira turned violent...

Ah! ça ira, ça ira, ça ira
les aristocrates à la lanterne!
Ah! ça ira, ça ira, ça ira
les aristocrates on les pendra!
Aristocrats to the lamp-post, the aristocrats, we'll hang them!

MUSIC In issues 134 and 135 of *Ancient Times,* 2012, the journal of The Company of Fifers & Drummers, Robin Engelman gives a thorough account of the evolution of the tune we know as *The Downfall of Paris.* Engelman traces its origins from the *La Carillon National,* to *Ça Ira,* to *The Fall of Paris* and finally to *The Downfall of Paris.*

In *Ancient Times,* *The Fall of Paris* is shown as having four parts; an A, B, C and D. This musical structure has carried forward to the Irish set dance tune we know today. According to historian Ken Purvis, *The Downfall* was written by British musicians as a parody of the French Revolutionary song *Ça Ira.* *The Downfall of Paris* set dance tune as played and danced today is included as a hornpipe in O'Neill (1903) and as a set dance in O'Neill (1907).

DANCE In the early 1960s, John Cullinane performed a set dance to the final two parts of *The Downfall of Paris* at the Feis Ceoil in Sligo. Even though the melody contains four parts, only the A and B sections are normally performed.

ILLUSTRATION The illustration is based on an etching from 1789 depicting Parisian militia carrying the severed heads of Governor de Launay and Mayor de Flesselles. Its caption reads 'C'est ainsi qu'on se venge des traîtres' (Thus we take revenge on traitors).

2/4 time signature

8 bars in step

16 bars in set

The Downfall of Paris — Trad

THE ACE AND DEUCE OF PIPERING

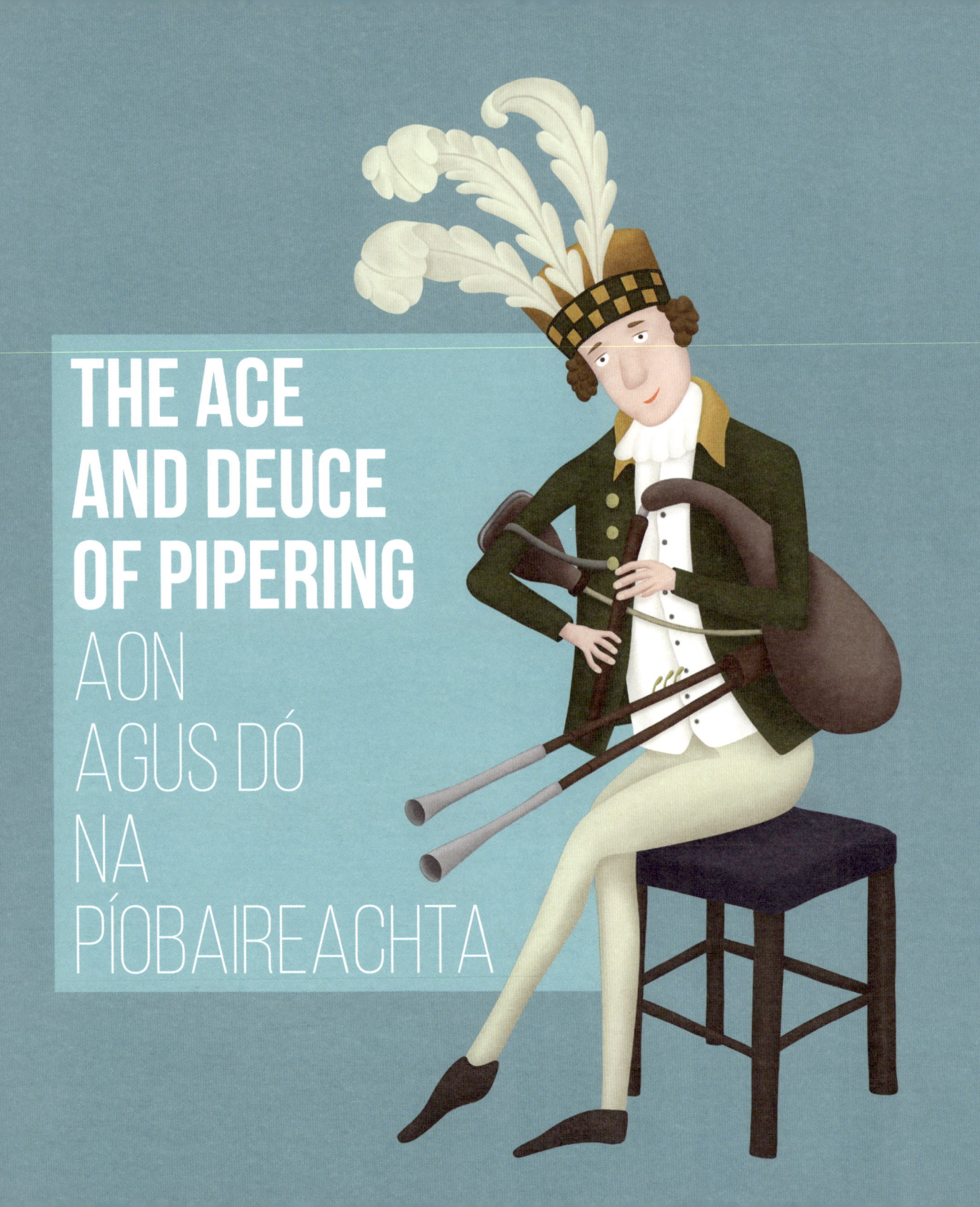

AON AGUS DÓ NA PÍOBAIREACHTA

BALLETIC PIPING

1791

STORY Ace is the lowest numbered side of a dice, the single dot, and comes from the Latin for 'unit'. After ace comes deuce, the old French word for two, then trey, cater, cinque, sice. The term 'ace and deuce' refers to first and second and came to mean 'the very best of' something.

Pipe playing in Ireland has two historical instruments, the píob mhór (referred to as 'warpipes' in English) and the uilleann pipes. Warpipes are an ancient mouth-blown instrument akin to the bagpipes (see *The Piper Through the Meadow Straying*, p47).

The uilleann pipes (or union pipes) are more recent and date from the early-eighteenth century. Unlike the warpipes, they use a bellows operated by the elbow to get their air, hence the name 'uilleann', the Irish for elbow. They also have a unique system of drones in three octaves, and regulators that enable a skilful player to accompany their own melody playing.

Dating from the mid-nineteenth century, *The Ace and Deuce of Pipering* is an intricate tune, and is regarded as a challenge to the skill of any piper. Those who play it well are the ace and deuce of pipers, the very best.

MUSIC *The Ace and Deuce of Pipering* is found in the Joyce (1873) and in Roche (Vol. 3, 1927). Joyce noted that it was transcribed in 1853 from the whistling of John Dolan from Gleann Oisín in Co. Limerick.

DANCE The structure of *The Ace and Deuce of Pipering* is unusual. Both the step and set parts (A and B) are composed of 12-bar phrases. In order to remember this, exam candidates for the CLRG teaching diploma (TCRG) often use a mnemonic 'Aon agus Dó', 1 and 2, to remind them of the equal 12-bar structure. In competition a musician will play the A part three times, followed by the B part once. The dancer will wait during the first A part and dance the step section during the second and third playing of the A part. The dancer will then dance the set to the single B part. Up until the late 1970s, the set part was also repeated if the adjudicator so wished.

ILLUSTRATION Many men and women could claim to be the best piper, but one particularly famous piper of old was the piper O'Farrell from Clonmel. He performed in London in 1791, as part of the ballet pantomime *Oscar and Malvina*. He published the first book of uilleann piping tunes in 1804. The title page featured an image of him performing Oscar and Malvina in elaborate costume. The image is redrawn here as our title illustration. O'Farrell gave his book this modest title...

4/4 time signature

12 bars in step

12 bars in set

O'FARRELL'S,
Collection of NATIONAL IRISH MUSIC *for the* UNION PIPES,
Comprising a Variety of
the Most Favorite Slow & Sprightly
TUNES, SET *in proper* STILE & TASTE
with Variations and Adapted Likewise
for the GERMAN FLUTE, VIOLIN, FLAGELET, PIANO
& HARP, *with a* SELECTION
of Favorite Scotch Tunes,
Also a Treatise with the most
Perfect Instructions everyet Published for the
PIPES.

The Ace and Deuce of Pipering — Trad

COMPOSERS

Some of the tunes contained in this book can be found in music collections spanning five centuries. Others are recently written and published. This section introduces some of the composers who contributed to the repertoire of set dance tunes.

For the tunes composed in the twentieth and twenty-first centuries, the composers are relatively easy to confirm. Recent compositions by Phelim Warren, Francis Ward and Michael Fitzpatrick have been included with their permission.

For older set dance tunes where a composer has been listed within the collections, some care needs to be taken. In some instances, a tune has been associated with more than one composer. There are a number of mitigating factors to consider.

For the main part, Irish traditional music is an oral tradition where tunes are passed on through listening and playing. In this context, acknowledgement of who originally composed a tune may be replaced over time by a reference to who passed on the tune.

A second factor to consider was the tendency of some collectors to copy from other manuscripts. Inexpensive and easily available manuscripts where sometimes republished without full attribution, resulting in a loss of clarifying detail.

Nationalistic fervour also played its part. An obsession with labelling a tune as Irish, English, Scottish or Welsh in origin resulted in some incorrect labelling.

TURLOUGH CAROLAN

1670-1738

Turlough Carolan was born in 1670 near the village of Nobber, Co. Meath. He went to school in Cruisetown where he encountered Bridget Cruise. She is said to have been his first love. When he was a teenager, the family moved to Connaught. Turlough's father started work as an ironmonger for the St. George family in Co. Leitrim, and later for the MacDermott Roe family in Kilronan, Co. Roscommon.

Turlough lost his sight when he caught smallpox at the age of 18. At that time, it was quite common for the visually impaired to study the harp as a profession. Thanks to the patronage of Mrs MacDermott Roe, he was afforded this opportunity. This led him to travel the country playing music and composing airs, planxties and poetry. He had many influential patrons whose names are immortalised in his tunes.

In his personal life, he was married to Mary Maguire and they had seven children. One son also became a harper and went to London to earn his living as a musician.

Although not known as a virtuosic performer of music, Carolan is famed for his excellence in composition. Almost 220 of his compositions are known today. His musical style could be described as Irish Baroque. He died in 1738, having been cared for during his final illness by Mrs, MacDermott Roe. He is reputedly interred in the McDermott Roe mausoleum in Co. Roscommon (O'Sullivan, 1958).

Set dance tunes attributed to Carolan are Miss Browne's Fancy (p23), Planxty Drury (p25) and Planxty Hugh O'Donnell (p27).

THE CONNELLAN BROTHERS

C. 1640-C. 1698

Thomas Connellan was a renowned Irish harper and composer. He was born in Cloonamahon, Co. Sligo c. 1640. He died in Lough Gur in Co. Limerick c. 1698. Evans Wentz (1909) gave an account of the local lore of Knockainey, Co. Limerick, which relates to the death of Connellan. His death was said to have been lamented and keened by the Goddess Áine who dwelled in the lake near Lough Gur (see *The Storyteller*, p81).

His younger brother, William Connellan, was also a notable harper and composer. William was sometimes referred to as Laurence and was born in Sligo in the mid-seventeenth century. They were well received in Scotland as well as in Ireland. Thomas Connellan was celebrated in Edinburgh after his death.

Some of the tunes attributed to the Connellan brothers include *Planxty Davis* (p19), *Fáinne Geal an Lae* and *Limerick's Lamentation*. The Connellan brothers were contemporaries of Carolan. The air *Molly McAlpin* was attributed to William Connellan. This particular air found favour with Carolan, who proclaimed that he would have traded all his airs to have composed this tune.

NATHANIEL GOW
C. 1763-1831

Nathaniel Gow was the fourth son of renowned Scottish dance musician Niel (or Neil) Gow. Niel is known to have composed several tunes. Nathaniel prepared his father's tunes for publication. He was also an acclaimed violinist and composer in his own right.

There is a lack of clarity as to which tunes were Nathaniel's compositions. This is due to a number of circumstances. As within Ireland, traditional repertoire in Scotland was largely passed on in the oral tradition in the eighteenth and early-nineteenth centuries. In this environment, tune attribution was somewhat inconsistent. Many tunes became known as Gow compositions, but authorship remained unclear. It is also rumoured that in his publications, Nathaniel claimed authorship of melodies that were composed elsewhere.

One of the set dance tunes credited to Nathaniel is *Miss Brown's Fancy* (p23). It is published in the Gow collection as *Miss Margrett Brown's Favourite*. However, the same tune has also been linked to Carolan. Nathaniel's son, Neil the younger, was also an accomplished violinist and composer of note.

WALKER 'PIPER' JACKSON
1716-1798

Gentleman piper Walker 'Piper' Jackson, came from the townland of Lisduan, near Aughrim Co. Limerick. He was an accomplished bagpiper and violinist and was also known as a prolific composer. A selection of his tunes appears in *Jackson's Celebrated Irish Tunes*, first published in Dublin in 1774 by Samuel Lee and reprinted in 1790 by Edmund Lee. Many of his compositions retain the name Jackson in the title. His brother Miles 'Hero' Jackson was a sheriff in Limerick in the mid-eighteenth century.

He is sometimes confused with another Jackson who hailed from Ballybay in Co. Monaghan. According to Bill Haneman (billhaneman.ie), there was a Jackson family in Ballybay who were landlords and of gentleman stock. Thus there may have been two families of Jackson composers. Some tunes attributed to Walker 'Piper' Jackson may have originated elsewhere.

Walker 'Piper' Jackson is said to have composed the *Humours of Listivain*, a related tune to *The Humours of Bandon* set dance (p13). He died in 1798.

DON O'DOHERTY
2008 *(deceased)*

Don O'Doherty was a well-known musician, composer, broadcaster and compere from Ireland's North West. With roots in Inishowen, O'Doherty lived in Derry. He was married to acclaimed Irish dance teacher Mary McLaughlin ADCRG, who was also a President of An Chomhdháil.

He toured America in the 1960s with the Taste of Ireland group and even got to perform on the famous *Ed Sullivan Show*. He was a leading light of the city's entertainment scene and a prominent figure in the running of Feis Dhoire Cholmcille (the Derry Feis).

He also ran the Irish shop in the Craft Village in Derry and often organised cultural events during the holiday season. He worked as a radio broadcaster for Radio Foyle and Highland Radio. In addition to his high profile role in the entertainments scene, O'Doherty is also remembered for his charity fundraising.

Three of the set dances in this collection were composed by O'Doherty. *The Four Masters* (p15), *The Storyteller* (p81) and *The Blue Eyed Rascal* (p85). *The Blue Eyed Rascal* was composed for his wife Mary.

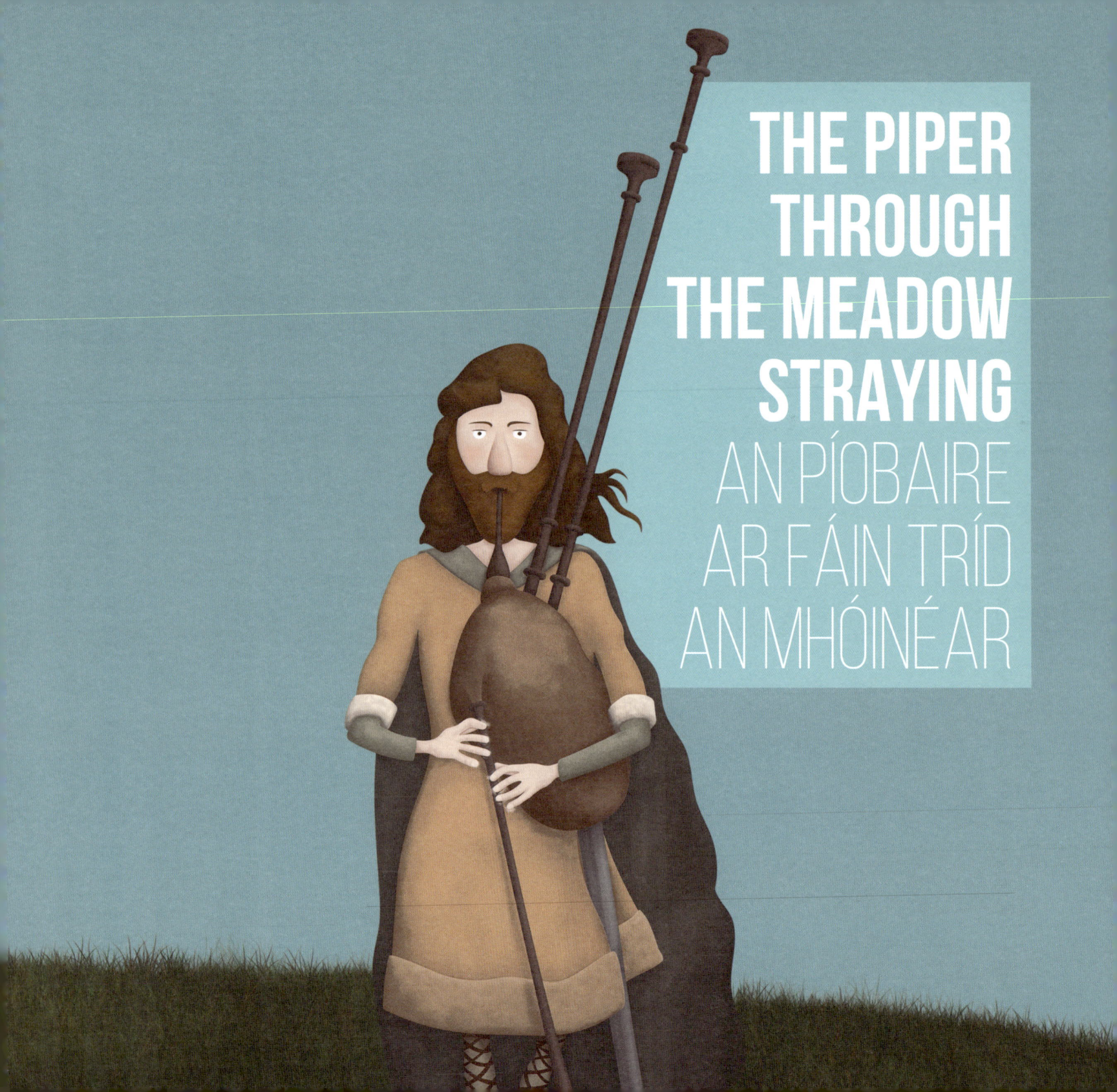

THE PIPER THROUGH THE MEADOW STRAYING

AN PÍOBAIRE AR FÁIN TRÍD AN MHÓINÉAR

'TWAS HIS WIFE THAT SPOIL'D HIS PIPING

1795

STORY In a case of 'the chicken and the egg', *The Piper Through the Meadow Straying* may get its name from a song in *Zorinski*, a 1795 ballad opera. Alternatively, the ballad may get its name from an existing tune of the time. Ballad operas started with *The Beggar's Opera* in 1728 and gained popularity as fun, satirical versions of high-society operas. They featured newly written comedic lyrics set to Irish, Welsh, Scottish, or even French folk tunes.

Zorinski tells the story of the adventures of a Polish king and his subjects, with a stereotypical Irish character thrown in for comedy. In Act 2, Scene 2, the melody we now know as *The Piper Through the Meadow Straying* is used for the duet of Polish peasant characters Witski and his wife Winifred. They have a lovers' tiff and then break into song, recalling their first meeting...

Winifred *A piper o'er the meadows straying,*
Met a simple maid a maying,
Straight he won her heart by playing,
Fal de ral, &c.
Wedded, soon each tone grew teazing,
Fal de ral, &c.
His pipe had lost the power of pleasing,
Fal de ral, &c.

Witski *Wedlock's laws are hard and griping,*
Women fretful – arts are ripe in,
'Twas his wife that spoil'd his piping,
Fal de ral, &c.
Her shrill note marr'd every sonnet,
Fal de ral, &c.
And crack'd his pipe, depend upon it,
Fal de ral, &c.

Zorinski: A Play, in Three Acts, 1795.

MUSIC The melody of *The Piper Through the Meadow Straying* almost certainly comes from the Welsh language song, *Nos Galan*, a traditional New Year's song. One of its earliest publications is within *British Harmony, Being a Collection of Ancient Welsh Airs* by John Parry, 1781. The melody of *Nos Galan* appears as the music for *Duet of Witski and Winifred* in *Zorinski*, 1795. The melody of *Nos Galan* was also used for the Chritmas carol *Deck the Halls**.

Within collections of Irish music, the same melody first appears under the title *A Piper O'er the Meadows Straying* in O'Farrell's *Collection of National Music for the Union Pipes*, 1804. Considering this is only a few years after the popularity of *Zorinski*, it is possible that the Irish version and the title stem from the ballad opera and not the other way around. Through O'Farrell, *The Piper Through the Meadow Straying* became a popular tune for uilleann pipe players, other musicians and dancers.

DANCE *The Piper Through the Meadow Straying* was one of several dances choreographed by dancer Brendan de Glin from Derry. In the early 1940s, he took a number of set dances from the O'Neill music collections and choreographed dances to fit the tunes (Cullinane, 1999).

ILLUSTRATION At the beginning of the twentieth century, the Gaelic League encouraged Irish industries to advertise in the Irish language, use the traditional Gaelic script (half-uncial) and display other symbols of Irishness. The illustration is based on a vintage advertisement for Goodbody's Píobaire cigarettes. The ad featured a Gaelic piper, standing in a meadow, playing the píob mhór.

HORNPIPE

4/4 time signature

8 bars in step

12 bars in set

* *From New Year to Christmas*

In 1862, Nos Galan appeared for the first time with English lyrics in *Welsh Melodies*, Vol. 2, by John Thomas. The English lyrics by Thomas Oliphan began with 'Deck the halls with boughs of holly...'. It moved the emphasis from the Welsh celebration of New Year to preparations for Christmas.

The Piper Through the Meadow Straying — Trad

47

THE JOB OF JOURNEYWORK
AN GREAS GIÚRNÁLA

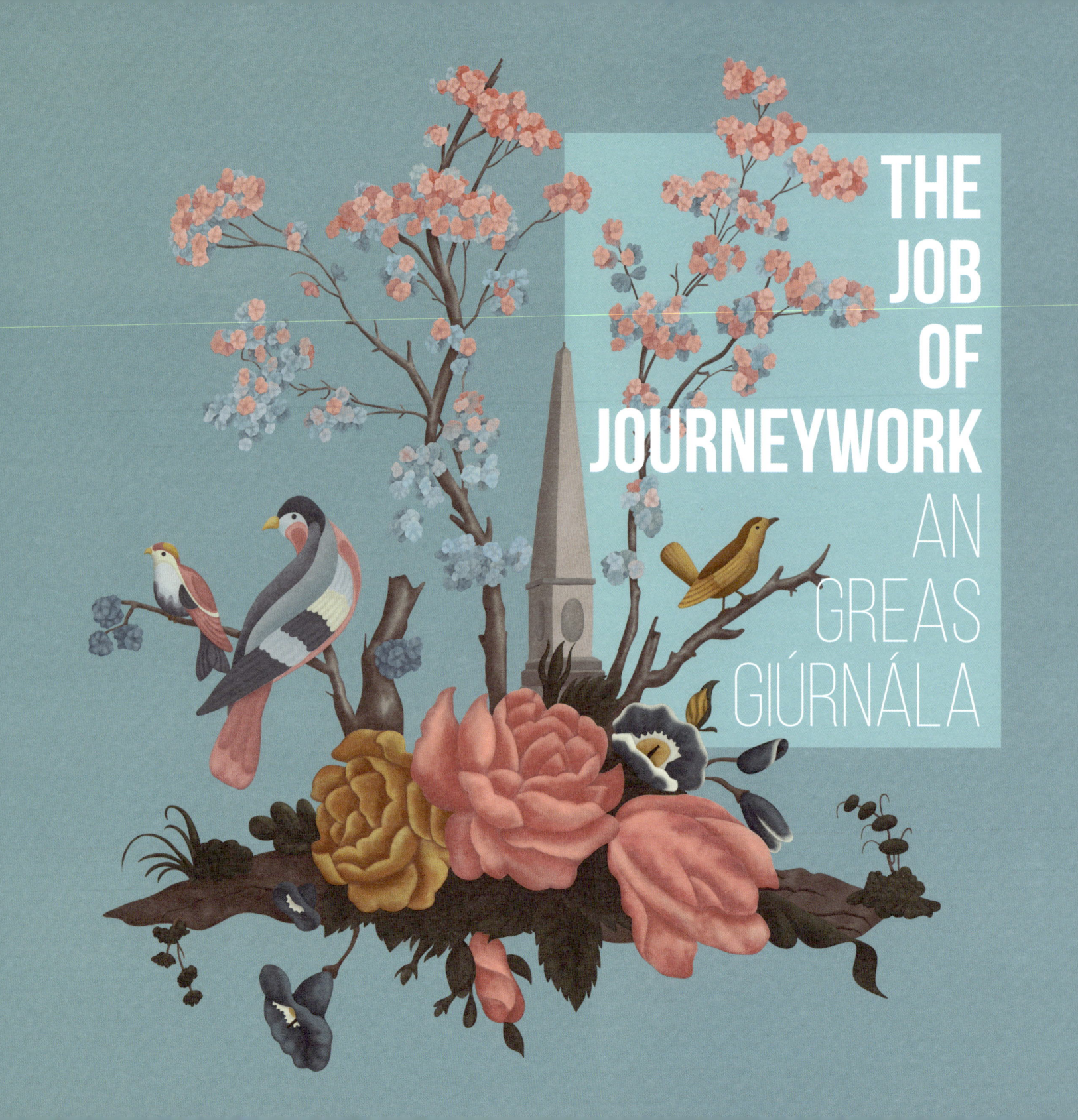

JOURNEYMAN CALICO PRINTER & UNITED IRISHMAN

1798

STORY In much of Europe during the Middle Ages, many crafts had systems of apprenticeship where years of training had to be completed before you were allowed to trade. During an apprenticeship, you would learn trade skills under the direction of a master craftsman. When your skills reached a level where your work was acceptable for hire or sale, you were granted the title of Journeyman. In many professions, you were then expected to journey as an itinerant professional, practising your skills throughout the country before you could aim for master level.

This journeyman system was introduced to Ireland from the time of the Tudor conquests. It was used in a wide variety of professions from carpentry, to tailoring, to wallpaper-making. Similar systems of training were also used in ancient Irish society. Years of apprenticeship were required before you could serve as a druid (pre-Christian priest), a brehon (expert in law), a file (oral historian), or a bard (poet and musician).

ILLUSTRATION The illustration for *The Job of Journeywork* is based on the Belvedere wallpaper pattern. This is regarded as one of the finest wallpaper designs produced in Ireland. Its design and manufacture is credited to James Smith, a paper-stainer and calico printer who was a Journeyman under Master Edward Clarke in Leixlip, Co. Kildare. Smith became a master papermaker and his designs adorn the walls of many of Ireland's finest houses.

Smith was also one of the merchant class sympathisers who was committed to the cause of the United Irishmen (see *The Drunken Gauger,* p35). In 1794, the United Irishmen movement was forced underground. They then planned a rebellion against British rule. The rebellion occurred over the summer of 1798. Based on the principles of The French Revolution, it aimed to establish an Irish Republic. The rebels failed in their attempt to launch a coordinated nationwide attack. The rebels were crushed and many of their leaders died in the aftermath. Smith was active in the military campaign in Kildare, and was arrested following his surrender in Sallins. He was imprisoned in Kilmainham Jail until 1802.

MUSIC This set dance was collected by Goodman c. 1860 and later published in Shields (Vol. 2, 2013). It appears in Joyce (1873), O'Neill (1903 & 1907) and Roche (Vol. 2, 1912). Joyce wrote that *The Job of Journeywork* was a great favourite in Munster.

A reel titled *The Job of Journey Work* appears in Aird (Vol. 3, c. 1795). This melody is used for the song *Here's His Health in Water* by the Scottish poet Robert Burns. Neither one is connected to *The Job of Journey Work* set dance.

DANCE There are several versions of this set dance associated with Munster, specifically a Limerick version and a Cork version. However, the version most commonly performed in Leinster is a combination of two old Cork steps, Curtin's Pick and Murray's. This version is accepted as the standard version for CLRG competition purposes.

The combined Cork steps probably became popular in Leinster through the dancing and teaching of Essie Connolly and Lily Comerford. These renowned dance teachers from Dublin are known to have travelled from Dublin to Cork to learn set dances from dancing master Cormac O'Keeffe. Essie learned *The Job of Journeywork*, *The Blackbird* and *The Garden of Daisies* from Mr O'Keeffe.

4/4 time signature

8 bars in step

14 bars in set

The Job of Journeywork — Trad

MADAME BONAPARTE

NOT TONIGHT JOSÉPHINE

1804

STORY Madame Bonaparte was born Marie-Josèphe-Rose Tascher de La Pagerie in 1763, on the French Caribbean Island of Martinique. When she turned sixteen, she was sent to Paris to enter into an arranged marriage with Viscount Alexandre de Beauharnais. They had two children, but the marriage failed and the couple separated.

When the French Revolution broke out (see *The Downfall of Paris*, p41), Viscount Beauharnais was arrested as an enemy of the state and, by association, so was she. The Viscount was guillotined on the 23rd July 1794, but while awaiting execution, Marie-Josèphe-Rose found her circumstances changed. The instigators of the Reign of Terror were themselves tried and executed. She was released five days after the Viscount's death.

Free at last, she lived life to the full. As a glamorous socialite, she had many affairs with high-profile men. In 1795, she met an up-and-coming army general, Napoleon Bonaparte. As he was six years her junior, she initially refused his advances, but his ongoing military success was a source of intrigue for her. Napoleon became infatuated and affectionately called her Joséphine.

After a whirlwind romance, they married in March 1796. Two weeks after the wedding, Napoleon was back on the battlefield. They saw little of each other over the following years but were able to correspond by love-letter.

Through success after success, Napoleon proved himself to be one of the world's greatest military commanders and rose to the highest rank in France. By 1804, much of Europe was under French control, and the French Senate proclaimed him Emperor. In a lavish ceremony officiated by Pope Pius VII, Napoleon was ordained as Emperor of France on December 2nd 1804. His wife, Madame Bonaparte, became Empress Joséphine. This signaled the beginning of the First French Empire.

Unfortunately, Joséphine was not able to conceive an heir for Napoleon and in a tearful divorce ceremony in January 1810, they parted ways. She lived out her days at Château de Malmaison, a vast estate outside Paris. She died in May 1814, probably of pneumonia.

MUSIC The melody of *Madame Bonaparte* is found in two of O'Neill's collections but under different titles. It is in *Music of Ireland* (1903) as *Bonaparte's Advance*, but in *Dance Music of Ireland* (1907) as *Madame Bonaparte*.

In *Stone Mad for Music*, 1999, Donal Hickey notes that *Madame Bonaparte* was in the repertoire of James Gandsey, an uilleann piper from Co. Kerry. Like Turlough Carolan, he had very poor eyesight due to smallpox, and he received patronage from a member of the aristocracy. He was affectionately known as 'Lord Headley's piper', and the 'The Killarney Minstrel'. He died in 1857 aged 90.

Celia Pendlebury in *Jigs, Reels and Hornpipes: A History of "Traditional" Dance Tunes of Britain and Ireland* says this tune is commonly played in the repertoire of Northumbrian pipers in the North East of England.

DANCE *Madame Bonaparte* is quite a short set dance for step dancers. It only has an 8-bar step part, while the set section is 12 bars long. This set was one of the dances performed by Áine Ní Thuathaigh from Limerick. Áine won the coveted Munster belt and the All-Ireland Championship in the 1950s.

4/4 time signature

8 bars in step

12 bars in set

Illustration

The illustration is based on the painting *Joséphine en costume de sacre* (Joséphine in coronation costume) by Baron François Gérard c. 1807. It shows Joséphine in her coronation regalia. The painting is part of the art collection at Château de Fontainebleau.

Madame Bonaparte — Trad

THE SPRIG OF SHILLELAGH
AN GÉAG SILÉALAIGH

STORY A sprig is a horticultural term for a young twig or branch of a plant. A shillelagh is a long stick, around a meter in length, made from a young tree-branch. Shillelaghs are a staple in most Irish tourist shops and often thought of as a walking stick. Historically, they were used for walking, but their main purpose was as a weapon for self-defense, or attack. Stick fighting was a common Irish sport for centuries, but had evolved into widespread gang fighting by the early-eighteenth century. (see *The Blackthorn Stick*, p59). Most modern Shillelaghs are made from branches of the Blackthorn tree, but other woods such as Ash and Oak were also used.

TWIGS, JOKES & MILITARY CAMPAIGNS

c. 1807

The Shillelagh gets its name from a historic Oak forest in Co. Wicklow, close to the town Shillelagh. The word Shillelagh can be traced back to the eighth century and the Síl nÉladaig clan from the line of the Uí Chennselaig (Kinsella) kings of Leinster. The descendants of the Síl nÉladaig settled where today's town of Shillelagh is found.

SONG *The Sprig of Shillelagh* is a ballad song set to the tune of an English Morris jig called *The Black Joak*. It was published as a broadside in 1807. The lyrics are attributed to Edward Lysaght, a police magistrate for Dublin.

The publication of *The Sprig of Shillelagh* coincided with the start of the Peninsula War. In 1807, Napoleon invaded Portugal with the aid of the Spanish. He then turned on the Spanish and occupied the whole of the Iberian Peninsula. Against the backdrop of Napoleon's invasion, the lyrics of *The Sprig of Shillelagh* called for Irish loyalty to Britain and for the nations of the United Kingdom to unite against French aggression.

Britain joined a coalition of countries allied against Bonaparte and landed troops in Portugal in August 1808. The British troops included the '27th Inniskillings', who adopted *The Sprig of Shillelagh* as their regimental march. Battalions of the 27th fought in many battles against Bonaparte's army. The 1st Battalion fought at The Battle of Waterloo (see *Bonaparte's Retreat*, p55). *The Sprig of Shillelagh* is still a well-known military march within unionist communities in Northern Ireland today.

> *Bless the country, say I, that gave Patrick his birth,*
> *Bless the land of the oak and its neighbouring earth,*
> *Where grows the shillelagh and shamrock so green;*
> *May the sons of the Thames, the Tweed and the Shannon,*
> *Drub the foes who dare plant on our confines a cannon,*
> *United and happy at loyalty's shrine,*
> *May the rose, leek and thistle long flourish and twine*
> *Round a sprig of shillelagh and shamrock so green*

Final verse of *The Sprig of Shillelagh*, Broadside: *Harding B 10(50), 1807.*

Ironically, the song's composer, Edward Lysaght, later joined the Irish Volunteers and opposed the Act of Union*.

MUSIC The melody of *The Sprig of Shillelagh* comes from an earlier song, *The Black Joak*. Written as a comic song, the lyrics of *The Black Joak* were crude and obscene, while the melody was very catchy. The 'black' in the title was in reference to hair colour. With several different spellings, the less said about what a 'joak' was, the better.

It gained great popularity across all sections of society in Ireland and Britain. One of the earliest printed versions is dated to 1729 in *The Beggar's Wedding*, a ballad opera by Charles Coffey where it is titled *Coal-Black Joak*. The catchy melody was used for country dancing, even in the Royal Court**. It also lent itself easily to the setting of new lyrics, including *The Sprig of Shillelagh* song. It appears as the *Spring of Shillelagh* in *The Irish Musical Repository*, by B. Crosby, 1808.

DANCE The earliest known dance setting of *The Sprig of Shillelagh* dates back to the 1850s. Cormac O'Keeffe learned a setting of this dance from Tadhg Riordan of Co. Cork. Cormac then passed this onto his pupils. Tadhg Riordan was a farmer from west of Macroom in Co. Cork. He was known as an excellent dancer in his youth. By the time he encountered Cormac O'Keeffe, he was quite advanced in years. Riordan taught O'Keeffe difficult steps and movements while holding onto a table or using a walking stick to keep his balance (Cullinane, 1999).

6/8 time signature

6 bars in step

10 bars in set

*** Act of Union**
Following the 1798 Rebellion (see *Job of Journey Work*, p49), the Parliament in Ireland was dissolved and the Act of Union was passed in 1800. This established the United Kingdom of Great Britain and Ireland. Ireland was ruled from Westminster until 1922 as a result.

**** Sonata in G major**
The Black Joak melody was reworked into 'art music' by the Italian composer Muzio Clementi in his *Sonata in G major, Op.1, No.3, 2nd movement - Air Anglais*.

The Sprig of Shillelagh — Trad

BONAPARTE'S RETREAT
CÚLÚ BONAPARTE

Il s'est sauvé de l'Egypte de Madrid de Moscou de Leipsic de Mont StJean

Vite à PARIS

ILLUSTRATION The illustration is a redrawing of an 1815 satirical etching held at The British Musuem. Created by Pierre Joseph Moithey, it commemorates Bonaparte's famous retreats. Its inscription translates as *The Caesar of 1815, I came, I saw... I fled*. While the English refer to The Battle of Waterloo, Bonaparte called it the La Bataille de Mont-Saint-Jean. The victor writes history.

JE SUIS VENU, J'AI VU... J'AI FUI
(I came, I saw... I fled)

1815

HORNPIPE

STORY Viewed from abroad, the French Revolution had set a dangerous precedent for European monarchies. The revolutionary forces had executed nobles and ultimately led to the creation of a French Republic in 1792 (see *The Downfall of Paris*, p41). It was a direct threat to their world order and needed to be suppressed. They formed a coalition and invaded.

As a brilliant military commander, Napoleon Bonaparte played a large part in defeating the coalition's incursions. He took power and invaded the coalition countries. By the early 1800s, he had conquered much of Europe. To the French, he was a hero and they crowned him Emperor. To the Irish, he was a great hope for freedom from British rule and the establishment of an Irish Republic. To the monarchies, he was a dangerous upstart.

His spectacular rise to power wasn't without defeat. In 1798, Bonaparte led an invasion of Egypt but was forced into retreat in 1801. In 1807, he started the Peninsular War by invading Portugal, then Spain. In Autumn of 1812 he invaded Russia. He reached Moscow, only to find the Russians had sabotaged their own capital. It was abandoned, emptied of food, and left burning. His massive army had little food or shelter in the harsh Russian winter and he was forced to retreat.

Back in Spain, a battle led by the British outside Madrid saw the French army defeated there. Bonaparte's run of luck was over. Pressing to defeat him once and for all, a coalition of Austrian, Prussian, Russian, and Swedish forces faced off against Bonaparte's troops at Leipzig. The battle raged for several days before Bonaparte's army was decisively beaten for the first time. Though his troops fell back to defend France, the coalition pressed forwards and captured Paris in 1814. The French Senate turned against Bonaparte and forced him to abdicate. He was exiled to the small island of Elba in the Mediterranean.

While on Elba, his ex-wife and the love of his life, Joséphine, died (see *Madame Bonaparte*, p51). While he was grieving, he conspired to take back France. He landed on the Côte d'Azur with 700 men, and a few months later, he was back on the French throne. His new reign was short-lived and only lasted 100 days. In 1815, the Congress of Vienna declared Bonaparte to be an outlaw and the armies of Austria, Great Britain, Prussia and Russia joined against him. On the 18th of June, 1815, the French faced the coalition at The Battle of Waterloo*, and lost.

Bonaparte abdicated for a second time and was exiled to Saint Helena, a remote windswept island in the Atlantic. This was his final retreat from the world. His health failed quickly in the damp conditions and he died in exile in 1821.

MUSIC *Bonaparte's Retreat* is one of a number of tunes in the Irish tradition that are titled in honour of aspects of the Napoleonic era. The melody of *Bonaparte's Retreat*, the set dance, was published in the Roche (Vol. 2, 1912). It appears in O'Neill (1907). It also appears in O'Neill (1903) set in a minor key, which makes it sound like a different tune. A recording of *Bonaparte's Retreat* is found in Parlophone's 1931-32 Irish catalogue featuring uilleann piper, William Andrews.

DANCE In 1928 Maggie Kane learned a version of *Bonaparte's Retreat* from Eva Broughal. Broughal was Tailteann Games champion in 1924**.

4/4 time signature

8 bars in step

20 bars in set

* *Tunes at Waterloo*

The British forces at The Battle of Waterloo included the 1st Battalion of the 27th Iniskillings. It is possible that their regimental march, *The Sprig of Shillelagh* was played on the battlefield that day (see *The Sprig of Shillelagh*, p53).

** *Tailteann Games*

An 'Olympics' of Irish sport and culture organised by the government of the Irish Free State in 1924, 1928, 1932.

Bonaparte's Retreat — Trad

[sheet music]

BONAPARTE'S RETREAT

THE THREE SEA CAPTAINS
AN TRIÚR CAPTAEIN MARA

UNITED KINGDOM OF GREAT BRITAIN AND IRELAND.

RUSSIAN EMPIRE

KINGDOM OF FRANCE

OTTOMAN EMPIRE

OTTOMAN EMPIRE

THE BATTLE OF NAVARINO
Plyos

OTTOMAN EMPIRE

DUBIOUS FOLKLORE

1827

STORY According to music and dance folklore, *The Three Sea Captains* is named after the commanders of The Battle of Navarino in 1827, Vice-Admiral Edward Codrington, Rear-Admiral Henri de Rigny and Rear-Admiral Lodewijk Heyden. They headed up the British, French, and Russian warships who faced an Ottoman armada at Navarino, on the south west coast of Greece.

The French Revolution of the late 1700s gave inspiration to people across Europe that change was possible. In Ireland, the United Irishmen pushed for a republic and home rule. In Greece, a secret society called Filiki Eteria formed to fight for Greek liberation.

At this point, Greece had been under the rule of the vast Ottoman Empire for over three hundred years. The empire was Islamic but tolerated other religions as long as their followers paid substantial taxes. These taxes impoverished the Greeks Orthodox Christians.

In the 1820s, the Ottoman Empire was busy fighting elsewhere. Filiki Eteria saw this as an opportunity to stage their rebellion in Greece. In 1821, the uprising started. The initial years saw gains for the Greek revolutionaries, but the Ottomans pushed back in 1825. This suppression caught the imagination of ordinary Europeans who put pressure on their governments to intervene.

Like the Greeks, the Russians were also Orthodox Christians. Russia saw the Greek uprising as an opportunity to aid its religious brothers. The other European powers did not want to see Russia gaining territorial advantage, so they joined the fight to keep a balance of power. British ships arrived off the coast of Navarino and called a temporary truce. It didn't last, and joined by the French and Russian ships, the 'three sea captains' engaged with the Ottoman Armada. The Ottomans were defeated, making The Battle of Navarino a key turning point in the Greek War of Independence.

While folklore often has its basis in fact, The Battle of Navarino actually happened about 30 years *after* the first publication of this set dance. Codrington, de Rigny and Heyden are probably not the three sea captains referred to in the tune title.

MUSIC The melody of *The Three Sea Captains* was first published in *John Lee's Collection of Country Dances for the Present Year 1791*, titled as *The Three Captains*. It is also present in *Thomson's Collection of the Songs of Burns, Sir Walter Scott et al*, 1822. The same melody appears in O'Neill (1907) titled as *The Three Captains*, *The Three Sea Captains* and *Willam Clark's Favourite*. It is possible that 'Three Captains' was renamed to 'Three Sea Captains' in honour of The Battle of Navarino, but that is conjecture.

DANCE In competition, *The Three Sea Captains* has been danced as an open set for many years. However, a traditional setting has recently been introduced in the accepted repertoire of CLRG. *The Three Sea Captains* now has a dual designation as both an open set and a traditional set.

6/8 time signature
8 bars in step
20 bars in set

The Three Sea Captains — Trad

THE BLACKTHORN STICK
AN MAIDE DROIGHNEÁIN

AN IRISH MARTIAL ART

1829

STORY For many hundreds of years, the Irish used a variety of sticks in a martial arts practice called *Bataireacht*. *Bata* is an Irish language word for stick or cudgel, with *Bataireacht* roughly translating as 'sticking'. In the main, this was a working-class practice, but it involved high levels of skill. It had professional teachers and many different styles of fighting.

Sticks were made from sprigs or small branches from the Blackthorn, Oak, Ash or Hazel trees. They ranged from two to four feet in length, with a variety of names for each length. The most well-known stick type was the Shillelagh, which was one of the longest sticks used (see *The Sprig of Shillelagh*, p53).

As shown in the illustration, the stick can be grasped at about a third of its length. This follows the Antrim Bata style, where the lower third acts as a counterweight to the top two thirds which are thrown forward with high energy. The other arm is used as a guard, which is unusual in weapons fighting.

Bataireacht came into disrepute when large-scale faction or gang fighting broke out in the eighteenth century. These may have started out as fights for sport, but gradually turned into grudge fights to settle feuds. It is these gang fights that started the phrase 'Fighting Irish'.

Morgan O'Conner describes a familiar stick-fighting scene in his poem *Description of the County of Kerry*, 1726…

> *Off go the hats and the coats, the fight begins,*
> *Some strike the heads, whilst others strike the shins;*
> *The winding cudgels around their foreheads play,*
> *They need no leaders to begin the fray.*

Extract from *Poems, Pastorals and Dialogues*, Morgan O'Conner, 1726.

At its worst, this developed into a guerrilla war between factions of labourers fighting against the farming middle class over land rents and rights. Hostilities subsided in the 1820s when Daniel O'Connell, a famous campaigner for Catholic rights, called for Irish unity. Writer W. R. Le Fanu described a peace meeting of two rival factions, the Reaskawallahs and the Coffeys, in Co. Tipperary, 1829.

> *They marched six deep in military order with music and banners, each man carrying as an emblem of peace, a green bough, the procession nearly two miles long. On its arrival in Newport in the presence of much joy and whiskey and in the presence of the priests a perpetual peace was established and never from that day did those factions meet again in battle.*

Extract from *Seventy Years of Irish Life* by W. R. Le Fanu, 1893.

The revival of the Gaelic games of hurling and football led to the decline of *Bataireacht* in the late-nineteenth century. *Bataireacht* is virtually unknown in Ireland today. It is kept alive by Irish diaspora families in North America who use styles such as Rince an Bhata Uisce Bheatha and Antrim Bata.

MUSIC The melody of *The Blackthorn Stick* set dance appears in *O'Farrell's Pocket Companion for the Irish or Union Pipes*, c. 1816, under the title of *The Roving Pedlar* in 3/4 time. The same melody appears in Roche (Vol. 2, 1912) as *The Blackthorn Stick*, written in 6/8 time. It is a set dance with only one part of 15 bars. According to Joyce (1873), there were a number of Irish airs with this unusual structure. *The Funny Tailor* tune also shares this structure (see *The Drunken Gauger*, p35). A jig called *The Blackthorn Stick* also appears in O'Neill's *Irish Folk Music*, 1910, but it is a melody unrelated to this set dance tune.

DANCE The Blackthorn Stick is a 15-bar, single part melody written in 6/8 time. In competition, as with Planxty Davis, the tune is played through once as an introduction, then twice more for the dancer's step section. It is then played once more for the set section.

6/8 time signature

15 bars in step

15 bars in set

Illustration

The illustration depicts a defensive stance from the style of Rince an Bhata Uisce Bheatha (Dance of the Whiskey Sticks).

The Blackthorn Stick — Trad

THE ROVING PEDLAR
AN MANGAIRE FÁNACH

The term "pedlar" means any hawker, pedlar, petty chapman, tinker, caster of metals, mender of chairs, or other person who, without any horse or other beast bearing or drawing burden, travels and trades on foot and goes from town to town or to other men's houses, carrying to sell or exposing for sale any goods, wares, or merchandise, or procuring orders for goods, wares, or merchandise immediately to be delivered, or selling or offering for sale his skill in handicraft.

Pedlars Act, 1871

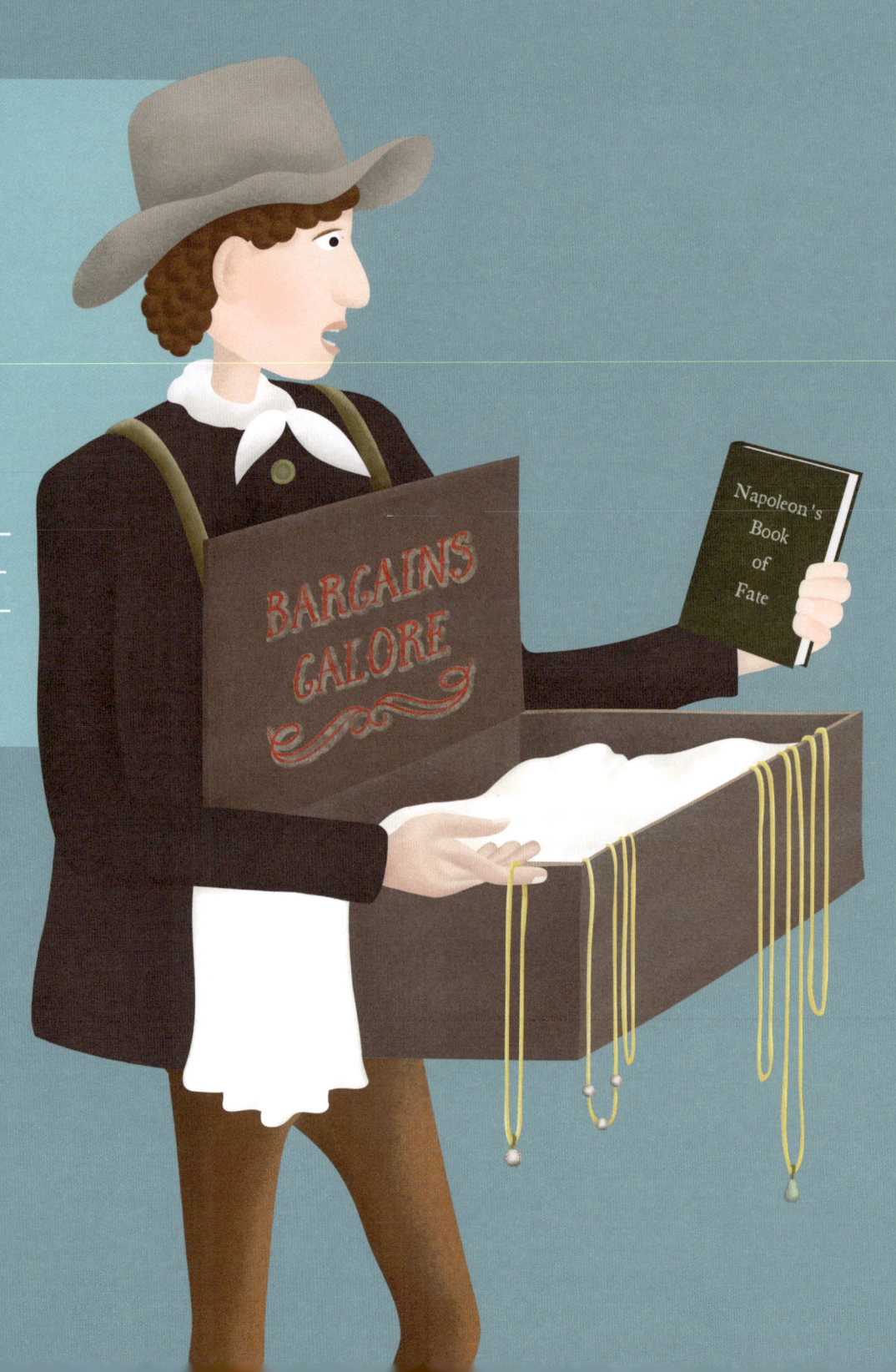

RAGS TO RICHES

c. 1830

STORY Pedlars and hawkers were small-scale merchants and craftspeople who travelled the countryside selling their goods door to door. The majority travelled on foot and sold anything that could fit within a backpack or sales box; books, ballad broadsides, clothing, tin pots or jewellery. A small number used a pack animal or hand-cart to increase the variety of goods they could offer. Others sold their services rather than goods. The dancing masters fitted into this category, although they may have considered themselves to be of higher status.
(see Dancing Masters, p66-67)

For rural communities, the arrival of a roving pedlar was an opportunity to access goods and services they couldn't find locally. Pedlars were viewed positively and were keenly anticipated. For shopkeepers, they were seen as having an unfair advantage and were unwelcome. Shopkeepers had to pay local taxes, whereas pedlars did not. As described in the Pedlars Act, however, pedlars did need to be licenced and pay fees in order to trade.

Pedlars were a source of interest for many fiction writers who would cast them either as clandestine smugglers and conspirators or as plucky entrepreneurs with rags-to-riches success stories.

One real-life rags-to-riches pedlar was James Duffy from Co. Monaghan. In the early 1800s, he was travelling the countryside as a pedlar selling prayer books. He is said to have noticed unwanted Protestant bibles given to Catholics and arranged to buy them on the cheap. He travelled to England and sold them for profit while buying a stock of books that would appeal back home. This trade brought in enough money for him to open a bookshop in Dublin, and later, to establish his own publishing house, James Duffy & Co. In the 1830s, he published *Napoleon's Book of Fate* to huge success. Better known as *Boney's Oraculum**, it was a book of fortune telling and was very popular. It got a mention in Seán O'Casey's play, *Juno and the Paycock*.

With first-hand experience of the market, Duffy published books and magazines with Catholic and nationalist themes that would appeal to a roving pedlar's customers. Each book had editions in different levels of quality and binding. His cheaply-bound books undercut the prices of other publishers and were within the price range of the rural poor. James Duffy & Co. also published the Grattan Flood edition of *Moore's Irish Melodies*. Moore wrote new songs to existing tunes, and his collection included songs set to the tune of *Saint Patrick's Day* and *The Black Joak* (The same tune used for *The Sprig of Shillelagh*).

MUSIC A tune called *The Roving Pedlar* appears in Petrie (1877) and O'Farrell (1804-16), but it is a melody unrelated to *The Roving Pedlar* as danced in CLRG competitions. *The Roving Pedlar,* the competition set dance, appears in *Dance Music of Ireland*, 1965, by Pat McNulty.

DANCE *The Roving Pedlar* is a relatively recent addition to the official list of set dances allowed in CLRG competitions. It was added in 2004. In competition, a dancer may request a set dance played at their preferred tempo. The slowest tempo allowed for set dances in hornpipe time is 76 bpm. *The Roving Pedlar* is most commonly heard played at these slow tempi for dance competitions and teacher exams. Sometimes it is played as a fast hornpipe set, but this is less common.

4/4
time signature

8
bars in step

14
bars in set

Boney's Oraculum
An internationally popular book giving instructions for fortune telling. It was supposedly discovered in an ancient royal tomb during Bonaparte's occupation of Egypt in 1801 and translated for him. It is claimed to have been used extensively by Bonaparte, and was amongst his possessions following his defeat at Leipzig in 1813.

The Roving Pedlar — Trad

THE ORANGE ROGUE
AN RÓGAIRE BUÍ

ORANGISM The winning of The Battle of the Boyne by William of Orange in 1690 sealed Protestant rule in Ireland. Penal Laws were enacted to prevent Catholics and Dissenters* from holding public office, teaching, owning firearms and more. A hundred years later, sectarian tensions between Catholics and Protestants were still ongoing.

In Co. Armagh, fighting erupted between Catholic and Protestant factions leading to the creation of the Loyal Orange Institution in 1795. Its aim was to protect Protestants and remain loyal to the British Crown. Its organisation was modelled on the Masons, complete with Lodges and Grand Masters. Membership expanded rapidly, gaining influence and spreading throughout the British Empire. Being Protestant in Ireland became synonymous with being 'Orange'.

SOLD OUT TO THE POPE

JIG

1836

STORY The origins of the word 'rogue' probably lie in Middle French where it meant arrogant or haughty. It came to mean someone who engaged in bad behaviour but was still likeable. Today, it equates to going against expected behaviour. In this sense, an orange rogue could be a member of the Orange Order who is badly behaved, but likeable, and goes against the grain. While we have no indication who was the original inspiration for this set dance, there is a historical figure who fits the bill.

Ogle Gowan was born in Co. Wexford in 1803 into a prominent family of Orangemen. He emigrated to Canada in 1829 and settled as a farmer. He observed the fractured Canadian Orange Order and used his political talents to establish the Grand Orange Lodge of British North America, later becoming its Grand Master. He ran for public office and was elected to the Legislative Assembly of Upper Canada in 1834.

His life was not without controversy. In *The Orangeman: The Life & Times of Ogle Gowan*, Ogle is summarised as…

…a bastard, a bigot and a brawler, yet his silver-tongued oratory and ruthless political skills made him more than a match for his enemies. Whether crossing swords with the fiery William Lyon Mackenzie or pub-crawling with the young John A. Macdonald he remained, always, slightly larger than life.
The Orangeman: The Life & Times of Ogle Gowan, Don Akenson, 1986.

He became a moderate within the Orange ranks when he formed an alliance with Catholics in his constituency. This helped him to gain his seat at the Legislative Assembly of Upper Canada for Leeds in 1836. This went against the grain. He later acknowledged Catholic loyalty during the Canadian Rebellions of 1837–1838. He was criticised by many as for having gone rogue and 'sold out to the Pope'.

He fell into disrepute in the 1860s when he was charged with criminal assault, but subsequently acquitted. In his later years, he became a liquor inspector, checking that the bars of Toronto were licenced. He died in 1876.

MUSIC A version of the melody was collected by Goodman c. 1860 and later published in Shields (Vol. 2, 2013) as *The Orange Rogue*. The A part of this version maps well to the set dance, but the B part is significantly different. A more related version of the melody appears in Joyce (1909) under the title *The Orangeman*. It is found in the *Jig* section of O'Neill (1903) and in the *Long Dance, Set Dance etc* section of O'Neill (1907).

DANCE According to Nellie Sweeney, Cormac O'Keeffe composed a setting of *The Orange Rogue* set dance while adjudicating a feis in Derry c. 1930. Nellie Sweeney was a dancer from Derry who was held in high regard. She informed Cullinane (2017) that, when she was young, her father did not allow her to learn hard shoe heavy jig or hornpipe steps. Apparently, this was the case for young ladies learning Irish dancing in Ulster early in the twentieth century.

6/8
time signature

8
bars in step

16
bars in set

Dissenters
Protestant denominations, like the Presbyterians, who dissented from the Anglican establishment church.

The Orange Rogue — Trad

STEEPLECHASE

The first race at Kilkenny was what is termed "a steeple-chase." This kind of race is of Irish origin, and has from thence extended all over the United Kingdom. Like all Irish sports, and Irish hunting, it has something especially wild in its character. It is said to have derived its name from a steeple, or some high object in the distance, being fixed upon as the point towards which the "high-mettled sons of Erin" ran their course, rushing straight forwards, headlong over stock and stone, hedge, ditch, wall, hill, and valley, until the appointed goal is reached.

Chapter XIX, *Travels in Ireland* by J. G. Kohl, 1844.

KILKENNY RACES
RÁSAÍ CHILL CHAINNIGH

STRAIGHT FORWARDS, HEADLONG OVER STOCK AND STONE

c. 1842

STORY The current racecourse in Kilkenny is Gowran Park, 15 kilometres to the east of Kilkenny city. Gowran Park opened in 1914, so it is not the race course from the time the *Kilkenny Races* set dance was composed. For that racecourse, we can turn to German travel writer, J. G. Kohl, who was travelling throughout Ireland in the years just before the Irish famine. In his book, *Travels in Ireland*, 1844, he describes his visit to the Kilkenny Races (c. 1842) in fascinating detail.

The racing festival lasted over three days and swelled Kilkenny's population from 25,000 to 40,000. The night before the races, the city's streets were filled with entertainers and people enjoying themselves. On the race day, Kohl travelled out of the city following the throng of people to the racecourse. The first race of the day was the steeplechase, Ireland's gift to horse racing and athletics.

The first steeplechase is said to have happened in Co. Cork in 1752. It was the result of a 'whose horse is faster?' bet between Edmund Blake and Cornelius O'Callaghan. They raced between Buttevant and Doneraile, using the furthest town's church steeple as the goal. This pitted horse and rider against whatever obstacles got in their way and quickly gained popularity as a highly challenging and exciting match race. Racing over open land had problems, so the format was changed to specific courses with purpose-built obstacles. This new format gained popularity and quickly spread to other countries.

A hundred years later, Irishmen were fighting as part of the Irish regiments of the Union Army during the American Civil War. To celebrate Saint Patrick's Day, they created a steeplechase course, announced as follows:

The prizes are a purse of $500; second horse to save his stakes; two and a half mile heat, best two in three, over four hurdles four and a half feet high, and five ditch fences, including two artificial rivers fifteen feet wide and six deep; hurdles to be made of forest pine, and braced with hoops.

Grand Irish Brigade announcement to Army of the Potomac, 1863.

A similar purpose-built steeplechase course would have been present at the Kilkenny Races during Kohl's visit.

MUSIC *Kilkenny Races* appears in Joyce (1909) with an instruction from the source, Mr. Victor Power, that it should be played 'with dashing vigour'.

The following 5 airs (with others) were sent to me by Mr. Victor Power of Leap Co. Cork, a good amateur violinist, with much knowledge of Irish music : about 1875.

Joyce (1909), p 97, referring to 5 airs, including *Kilkenny Races*.

It also appears in McNulty (1965).

DANCE When the *Kilkenny Races* is danced it often includes motifs which depict horse movements to reflect the title. Due to its length, a degree of fitness and athleticism is required for dancers who perform this set dance. In 1945 Cormac Mac Fhionnlaoich featured a musical setting of the *Kilkenny Races* on his radio show. Using this music, dance maestro Brendan de Glin choreographed a set dance for dancer and musician Eugene O'Donnell from Derry.

4/4 time signature

8 bars in step

24 bars in set

Kilkenny Races — Trad

DANCING MASTERS

This section introduces some of the dancing masters known to have composed the dances we dance today.

Itinerant dancing masters contributed significantly to the cultural fabric of rural Ireland in the eighteenth and nineteenth centuries. There are many records of their popularity in Munster counties and also along the east coast of Ireland. The dancing masters travelled throughout their local region, sometimes accompanied by a fiddle player. They stayed in an area for a period of six weeks teaching dance to all levels of society. They also focused on deportment and social etiquette. Some dancing masters assumed a French version of their name to heighten their perceived authority. At the end of the six weeks, they would have a Benefit Night; a concert event where the dancing master received payment (Foley, 2013).

The dancing masters all had their own repertoire and composed the steps to many of the traditional set dances we have today. They were territorial and keen to keep their students. Indeed, they reputedly held dance-offs to acquire a particular patch of the county. Many of the dancing masters were male although there is a record of a female dancing master from Kerry. She was affectionately known as 'Máirín a' Rince', Máirín of the dance (Brennan, 1999). She taught classes in Kerry and the surrounding counties in the late-nineteenth century.

In a modern context, the dancing master tradition lives on through teachers who travel the world choreographing new settings to set dance tunes.

O'KEARIN

LATE 1700S- EARLY 1800S

O'Kearin was a legendary dancing master from Castlemaine in south Kerry. He taught across Co. Kerry in the late-eighteenth and early-nineteenth centuries.

According to dance historians O'Keefe and O'Brien (1902), he provided order and uniformity within the Irish step dance canon. Francis O'Neill (1913) referred to him as a 'genius' for creating a system of Irish dance based on precise fundamental movements.

Among his pupils, who were mostly older adult males, was the father of renowned Kerry dancing master Professor P. D. Reidy. Reidy later taught dancing in London and was central to the preservation of repertoire promoted by the Gaelic League (Foley, 2013).

O'Kearin also taught 'Múirín na Rince', better known as Mooreen, who was noted for his skill in improvisation. Mooreen in turn taught Neidín Batt Walsh, a skilled technician who passed on his skills to Jeremiah Molyneaux.

MOLYNEAUX

1883 - 1967

Jeremiah Molyneaux, also known as Munnix, was a highly acclaimed Irish dance master from Co. Kerry. Fellow Kerryman Diarmaid Ó Catháin, affectionately called him the 'Michael Coleman of Irish dancing', such was the esteem in which he was held. Munnix was born in 1883. From Gunsboro, north of Listowel in Co. Kerry, he attended dance classes with Neidín Batt Walsh as a young boy. In 1903, he taught his first class and went on to teach dance throughout Kerry for a period that spanned 50 years.

He travelled the countryside accompanied by a musician and was an exacting perfectionist as a teacher. He would stay in an area for a period of up to six weeks. At the end of that time, he would hold a Benefit Night to receive payment for himself and his musician.

Molyneaux remained outside of the Gaelic League structured classes and thus retained control over his repertoire and choreography (Foley, 2013). He had a certain portion of his repertoire which he was reluctant to share and sometimes instructed the musician to play faster so that other dancers present would not be able to pick up his favourite steps.

He taught Phil and James T. McKenna who later emigrated to New York. James taught alongside dancing teacher Jerry Mulvihill, a native of Moyvane, Co. Kerry (Phelan, 2014).

Some of the Molyneaux repertoire is still danced at step dance competitions today. His settings of *The Blackbird* (p29) and *Saint Patrick's Day* (p7) are designated trad sets and are allowed for competition. The style his steps are danced with today may be quite different from his own, given the uniformity required for competition success. Molyneaux died in February 1967 and is buried in Gale cemetery.

THE MURRAY BROTHERS

1884 - 1948 *(Freddie)*

Cork brothers Freddie and Willie Murray made a tremendous contribution to the Irish dance repertoire now considered to be traditional. They came from a large family and lived in Sunday's Well in Cork city. Their influence was felt across Cork, Kerry, Waterford and England (Cullinane, 1999).

Freddie Murray was born in 1884 and worked in the building trade. Dancing was his passion and he was known to teach dancing at any occasion or location. When on holidays in Ardmore, he taught the O'Meara sisters from Clonmel. He enjoyed dancing to the music provided by Maureen O'Meara, who played violin. With other musicians, he was known to ask them to slow down if they played too quickly.

In the period between 1916 and 1921, a time of unrest in Ireland, Freddie was imprisoned three times. During his internment in the Curragh, he continued to share his steps with other dancers who were also incarcerated there. These dancers included Mr Lambe from Ballina Co. Mayo, father of Maura and Paddy Lambe, and a Mr Coleman from Galway.

Freddie's brother Willie was also a talented dancer. He emigrated to London in the late-1890s and worked as a bricklayer. He taught the Munster dances along with fellow Corkman Jack O'Brien.

The Murray brothers are thought to have learned some steps from Din Moore and Steve Comerford although structured classes were not in place at that time. Among the dances attributed to the Murrays are the traditional version of *The Garden of Daisies* (p5) and the step of *The Job of Journeywork* (p49). Both are still danced today.

CORMAC O KEEFFE

1896 - 1984

Cormac O'Keeffe was born in Barrack Street in Cork in 1896. He joined the Irish dancing class attached to the Cork Pipers' Club in 1902 while still a young child. The club was founded in 1898 by Sean Wayland, a native of Tipperary residing in Cork. Many musicians and dancers visited and taught at the Cork Pipers' Club. These included the Murray Brothers, Din Moore and Stephen Comerford. Tadhg Riordan and Jim Moynihan were among some of the older dancing masters who shared some of their steps with O'Keeffe.

O'Keeffe achieved success as a competitor and became the dance instructor at the Cork Pipers' Club in 1917. This preceded the establishment of An Coimisiún. Teachers from all over the country came to him to learn set dances. The late Una Ní Ruairc came from Limerick in 1940 and learned the traditional setting of *King of the Fairies* (p1) from him. Following the Tailteann Games in 1924, O'Keeffe contacted all the teachers and feis organisers in Cork and established the Cork Teachers Association, a branch of which is still active today.

RUB THE BAG
CUIMIL AN MÁLA

RÍRÁ, RUAILLE BUAILLE AGUS CUIMIL AN MÁLA

1855

STORY Rírá agus ruaille buaille is an Irish phrase that translates roughly as 'great noise and commotion'. It is often used to describe a crowd having a raucous and rowdy good time. In Munster, the phrase cuimil an mála means the same thing. It translates as 'rub the bag'.

It is worthy of remark, that the Munster name of this tune (Kimel-a-vaulen, as it is pronounced) is used, like "Ree Raw," to signify confusion or uproarious merriment.

Joyce, Ancient Irish Music, 1873.

It is probable that the bag being rubbed was the air bag of the uilleann pipes. The bag is squeezed by the elbow as the pipes are played. Many songs about Irish 'uproarious merriment' include mention of a piper and the pipe's bag.

Between 1845 and 1851, Ireland suffered a devastating famine. A huge portion of the Irish population was reliant on the potato as their primary food source. When a blight affected the potato crop for several years in a row, over a million people died. Nearly two and half million more emigrated to escape poverty and death. A vast number set sail for America, never to return. In cities like New York, the impoverished Irish congregated in areas of cheap accommodation, creating ghettos where Irish life continued on in a new land. They brought their music and dance with them, along with less welcome customs like faction fighting (see *The Blackthorn Stick*, p59).

On the American stage, the Irish were depicted using a variety of stereotyped characters, from being poor-but-noble to drunks and quick-tempered fighters. Many stage-Irish songs of the period start with an Irish party full of rírá agus ruaille buaille, followed by a fight. *Lanigan's Ball* is a famous example of this…

Whin we got there they were dancing the Polka,
All round the room in a quare whirligig;
But Kitty and I put a sthop to this nonsinse,
We tipt thim a taste of a nate Irish jig;
Oh! Mavrone, was'nt she proud of me,
We "bather'd the flure" til the ceiling did fall,
For I spent three weeks at Brooks' Academy,
Larning a step for Lanigan's ball.

Och! Arrah boys but thin was the ruptions,
Meself got a wollop from Phelim McCoo,
Soon I replied to his nate introduction,
And we kicked up the divil'd own phililaloo,
Casey the piper, he was nearly strangled,
They squeezed up his bags, chaunters and all;
The girls in their ribbons all got entangled,
And that put a stop to Lanigan's ball!

Verses three and five of *Lanigan's Ball*, 1863 original version.

MUSIC The *Rub the Bag* melody is found in Petrie (1855) titled as *Righ an Ratha* (*Rí na Rátha*). It is also in Shields (Vol. 1, 1998) as *Cuimil a Mháilín*. In those settings, the A part is quite similar to today's set dance tune, but the B part is quite different. The setting closest to the version used for the set dance today is *Cumail a Mháilín* as published in Joyce (1873).

DANCE Joyce (1873) noted that he learned the *Rub the Bag* tune in Limerick in the 1840s. He recalled seeing a man dance it on a table top, reflecting the 'uproarious merriment' of rírá agus cuimil an mála. *Rub the Bag* was introduced as a set dance at a feis organised by the Cork dance teachers in the late 1960s.

6/8 time signature

8 bars in step

14 bars in set

Illustration

The illustration is based on depictions of uilleann pipers in paintings such as *The Limerick Piper* by Joseph Patrick Haverty, 1844. The dancer is based on a character from *Children Dancing at the Crossroads*, a painting by Trevor Thomas Fowler, c. 1835, on display at the National Gallery of Ireland.

Rub the Bag — Trad

THE LIPS THAT TOUCH LIQUOR SHALL NEVER TOUCH MINE

THE LODGE ROAD BÓTHAR AN LÓISTE

JOYS & TEMPERANCE

1874

HORNPIPE

STORY There are several roads in Ireland called the Lodge Road. The one with perhaps the most interesting story is the Lodge Road in Belfast city.

Belfast's original Lodge Road dates from the early 1800s. Local historians describe it as the laneway to The Lodge, a mansion built by the Joy family. The Joys made their money from founding the *Belfast News Letter,* and although Protestant, had a great interest in Irish traditions. Henry Joy was one of the organisers of the Belfast Harp Festival of 1792, which helped to preserve much of the traditional harp music that we have today (see Bunting within Composers, p20).

Henry's nephew, Henry Joy McCracken, was a Protestant Irish Nationalist. He was a founding member of the Society of United Irishmen, along with William Drennan (see *The Drunken Gauger,* p35) and Wolfe Tone. The United Irishmen called for an independent Irish Republic and were inspired by the French Revolution (see *The Downfall of Paris,* p41). Joy McCracken led the Antrim uprising of the 1798 Rebellion against the English Crown (See *The Job of Journeywork,* p49).

The Lodge Road became the Old Lodge Road when a rival New Lodge Road was built a mile away. By the mid 1800s, the Old Lodge Road was a well-established neighbourhood.

A temperance movement flourished in Ireland in the 1830s. It was highly influential in its efforts to lower the consumption of alcohol. It was supported by religious leaders from the Catholic and Protestant faiths*. In Belfast, the Irish Temperance League (ITL) formed and campaigned for abstinence, through posters and song. The movement spread to America, and in 1874, a San Francisco songbook, *Temperance Songs and Chorus*, published *The Lips That Touch Liquor Shall Never Touch Mine*. In Belfast the same year, the ITL opened their first public café, offering an alcohol-free social space. A café kiosk was later opened on the Old Lodge Road, selling coffee, soda cake, and sandwiches.

The Old Lodge Road was bulldozed in the 1980s to make way for an urban motorway.

MUSIC *The Lodge Road* melody danced to in competition appears in O'Neill (1903 & 1907). It also appears in Roche (Vol. 3, 1927), but in that version, only the A part is the same. The middle of the B part is quite different to O'Neill's version. In *Sources of tunes in O'Neill's Music of Ireland and Dance Music of Ireland* (Unpublished, 2017) Paul de Grae relates that *The Lodge Road* was collected by James O'Neill for the Francis O'Neill music collections. De Grae suggests that *The Lodge Road* has hints of classical influences, possibly related to James O'Neill's experience as an orchestral violinist.

DANCE *The Lodge Road* is danced at the minimum metronomic tempo of 76 bpm, and also at faster hornpipe tempi. It is popular with dancers due to the length of the set section, the B part. The metronome was first introduced to the competitive Irish dance scene in Ireland in the 1980s. It helped regulate the tempo for set dances. Prior to that, teachers and dancers would wave frantically in order to communicate to the musician that they wished the tempo to be altered.

2/4 time signature

8 bars in step

20 bars in set

*****Faith Leaders**

Fr. Theobald Mathew founded the Teetotal Abstinence Society in 1838. Years later, in 1898, the Pioneer Total Abstinence Association was established by James Cullen. Many Orange lodges were temperance halls where consumption of alcohol was prohibited.

The Lodge Road — Trad

THE VANISHING LAKE

LOCH AN RITH AMACH

Loughareema! Loughareema
Lies so high among the heather;
A little lough, a dark lough,
The wather's black an' deep.
Ould herons go a-fishin' there,
An' sea-gulls all together
Flaot roun' the one green island
On the fairy lough asleep.

Loughareema, Loughareema;
When the sun goes down at seven,
When the hills are dark an' airy,
'Tis a curlew whistles sweet!
Then somethin' rustles all the reeds
That stand so thick an' even;
A litte wave runs up the shore
An' flees, as if on feet.

Loughareema, Loughareema!
Stars come out, an' stars are hidin';
The wather whispers on the stones,
The flittherin' moths are free.
One'st before the mornin' light
The Horsemen will come ridin'
Roun' an' roun' the fairy lough,
An' no one there to see.

The Fairy Lough, Songs of the Glens of Antrim
by Moira O'Neill, 1900

HERE TODAY, GONE TOMORROW

1898

JIG

STORY In Ireland's North East lie the Glens of Antrim, a beautiful series of valleys sweeping down to the sea. Taking the coast road from Cushendall to Ballycastle gives stunning views. Scotland is visible just 19 kilometres away. However, it's a narrow, twisty, dangerous road. In theory, taking the inland road is a safer and quicker route.

On an isolated stretch roughly half-way between Cushendall and Ballycastle, the inland road passes through a brown, peaty landscape. On other days, the same road passes through a lake. This is Loughareema, from the Irish *Loch an Rith Amach* (The Lake that Runs Out). The landscape is dry for much of the time, but when heavy rains fall, Loughareema fills. It can take as little as twelve hours for the waters to reach up to 20ft deep. A few days later, the lake may have vanished again.

The hills around Loughareema are impermeable rock, so waters run overland. When they reach Loughareema, they pass into a karst landscape of Cretaceous Chalk. Here, the land is permeable, and the waters drain through cracks and caves. If rains falls heavier and faster than the cracks and caves can drain, the lake appears and fills.

On September 30th, 1898, Colonel John Magee McNeil was in a hurry to catch a train. He needed to get from Cushendall to Ballycastle. The quickest route was the inland road, but it had been raining heavily for days. As his horse-drawn carriage approached Loughareema they found the road submerged. Coaxing the coachman to continue, they inched into the cold waters. As the horses got deeper and deeper, they took fright. A whip from the coachman and one of the horses reared up. When it came down, it dragged the carriage sideways, pulling it off the submerged roadway and into the deeper waters. The Colonel never made it to his train. Local legend says that a ghostly horse-drawn carriage can often be seen on the road through Loughareema.

MUSIC In 2012, the Marie Duffy Foundation put out a call for new set dance compositions. The Foundation supports creativity and innovation in Irish culture through awards for performers and choreographers. The Foundation wanted to propose something new to add variety to the set dance repertoire. A gala evening was held where live performances of the compositions were judged. The winning tune was *The Vanishing Lake*, by Francis Ward from Antrim. The set dance has a beautiful haunting melody, reflective of moody Loughareema. Francis is an accomplished traditional pianist and dance performer, and a well-known dance teacher with Scoil Uí Ruairc*. The set dance was added to the official list of CLRG in June 2012.

DANCE *The Vanishing Lake* is a very popular set dance on the competition stage. It challenges the stamina of the dancer given that the step part is 14 bars long, while the set part is 18 bars in length.

6/8 time signature

14 bars in step

18 bars in set

*** World Titles**

Francis Ward also has the distinction of choreographing settings of *The Vanishing Lake* for two of his students, Zoe Griffin and Ronan O'Brien. Both dancers won world titles performing his choreography to the melody he composed.

The Vanishing Lake — Francis Ward

IS THE BIG MAN WITHIN?
AN BHFUIL AN FEAR MÓR ISTIGH?

A THOROUGH-PACED RAKE

STORY 'Is the big man within?' is the kind of question a man might have asked the woman of the house when calling to her door. It's likely that the theme of this set dance, if not the tune, is related to songs such as *An Táilliúir Aerach (The Merry Tailor)* and *Bean an Fhir Rua (The Red-Haired Man's Wife)*. These tell stories of journeymen tailors and their reputation for getting young ladies into trouble.

In *Songs of the Irish*, 1960, Donal O'Sullivan describes these situations along the following lines. A man from the country might buy material for clothes at fairs or from roving pedlars, but have no means to make the clothes. He would wait for an itinerant tailor who would be invited to stay in the house while the clothes were tailored. While the man of the house went to work, the tailor was at home with the man's wife or daughters. It seems that plenty of tailors took advantage of the situation.

SONG There are several different *Táilliúir Aerach* songs, but all follow the same theme. Here is a verse from the singing of Mánus Ó Creag...

Oh, I am a light-hearted tailor with an interest in fun,
I would flirt with my darling when I had the chance,
There isn't a coastal town I would visit
Where I would not get a nice young maiden for a bottle of ale.

Translation of the first verse of *An Táilliúir Aerach* from the singing of Mánus Ó Creag in Donegal. Recorded by the Royal Irish Academy in 1935.

A different *Táilliúir Aerach* song was published in *The Journal of the Irish Folk Song Society* in 1924. This song is said to have been composed by Conchubhar Máistir Ó Ríoghbhardáin (c. 1770-1840). It paints an even worse picture of a rakish tailor...

They keep on saying that I am a thorough-paced rake,
And no good to the grass I stand on,
A terror among women, bringing sorrow to hundreds of them,
And ever a champion in every vulgar brawl,
Sitting in the publichouse without clothes to cover me,
Naked, teased and tormented among the crowds,
Without aim or object, without sufficiency or livelihood,
With no endowment of wits - a perfect fool.
When next morning I find this place has not a drop left,
I must be provided with a mount.
Oh! how my heels stick up when I lie in the bushes!
And what knocks I give my head against the walls!
But I am not content till I reach Gort na Péiste,
Nor would I go back to my shop to prepare my threads.
Thus I go running about from tavern to tavern;
Thus I profess and practice the merry life.

Translation of the first and third verses of *An Táilliúir Aerach*, from the *Journal of the Irish Folk Song Society* 21, 1924.

Published in the original Irish, several lines of the fifth verse were blanked out because they were seen as being too rude and bawdy*.

MUSIC *Is the Big Man Within?* appears in Roche (Vol. 2, 1912) titled as *Fear Mór*. It is also found in O'Neill (1907) as *Is the Big Man Within?*. *Is The Big Man Within?* is particularly unusual as the step part (A) is written in 9/8 or slip jig time, while the set part (B) is written in 6/8 or double jig time.

DANCE *Is the Big Man Within?* is the only set dance currently performed in Irish dance competitions to have a dual time signature. In 1981, the sheet music for this set dance was published in *Céim*, the CLRG publication. This was a conscious attempt to encourage more dancers to perform this in competition. Despite this, it is still rarely danced at feiseanna.

9/8 - 6/8 time signature

8 bars in step

8 bars in set

* bad company

The watered-down English translation given was:

Sheela telling Mary
that she was
a low woman,
Haunting the barracks
and quays
And keeping
bad company.

Is the Big Man Within? — Trad

THE FIDDLER 'ROUND THE FAIRY TREE

AN FIDLÉIR THART AR AN GCRANN SÍ

CEOL DRAÍOCHTA - MAGIC MUSIC

c. 1910

STORY Irish fairies are not the same fairies as found in other cultures. They don't have wings or wands. Irish fairies are the Aes Sídhe from Celtic mythology, the people of the mounds (See *King of the Fairies*, p1). The lore says they were the Tuatha Dé Danann, a race of supernatural humans. When the Gaels came to Ireland, the Tuatha Dé Danann were overwhelmed. They retreated to the Otherworld. There has been an uneasy truce since.

The entrances to the Otherworld are said to be through ringforts, mounds, or trees like lone Hawthorns. These fairy forts and fairy trees dot the landscape. According to the Creideamh Sí, the Fairy Faith, the fairies are highly protective of their property and can seek revenge on anyone who is disrespectful or causes damage. There are numerous folk stories about people who have harmed a fairy tree and have suffered dire consequences.

The flip side of the fairies is that they can also bring great good. At fairy trees and forts, people have left offerings or tied strips of cloth to branches as wishes for good fortune. There are many stories of people gaining great skills or abilities, all attributed to the fairies.

An example of this is a story about the famous Sligo fiddle player, Michael Coleman. In *Sligo Folk Tales*, 2015, Joe McGowan relates how other musicians described Coleman's exceptional music. To the piper Willie Clancy, Coleman's music sounded like 'Ceol Draíochta', magic music. To fiddle player Fred Finn, Coleman's music was literally *from* the fairies. Micheal Coleman had a brother, Jim, who was also a fine fiddle player. Jim told Fred's father the story of how they got their intricate music.

In this story, Micheal and Jim Coleman had been out for the night and were on their way home. They came across the local fairy fort and rested there awhile. Suddenly, they felt themselves to be somewhere else, surrounded by a beautiful landscape.

Feeling a compulsion to play they uncased their fiddles, sat down on a stone and started into a few tunes. They played on and on all night long as if enchanted and then, tired of playing, they set out again to find their way home.

Sligo Folk Tales by Joe McGowan, 2015.

From that night on, it was said that their fiddle playing was vastly improved. Over time, Jim stayed a local man, but Michael emigrated, first to England and then to America in 1914. His musical mastery was soon noticed and in 1921, his recording career began. Coleman recorded approximately eighty 78 rpm records for labels from Decca to Pathé and Columbia. His flamboyant, fast fiddle playing is still greatly admired and emulated today.

MUSIC The Fiddler 'Round the Fairy Tree melody appears in Joyce (1873) as *Farewell to the Troubles of the World*. It is found as *Farewell To My Troubles* in O'Neill (1903). The melody is published as *Fiddler Round the Fairy Tree* in *Music from Ireland*, Vol. 2, by D. Bulmer & N. Sharpley, 1974.

DANCE In the early 1960s, John Cullinane (1999) popularised this set dance in Munster. He interpreted the melody through an innovative choreography. He recalls performing it on request at feiseanna in Limerick while accompanied by local fiddler Cáit Ní Chúis.

6/8 time signature

8 bars in step

12 bars in set

Fiddler 'Round the Dance

Violinist May Keogh O'Brien was the official accompanist at major events organised by CLRG for many years. She was a legendary figure in the world of Irish dance. She had the distinguished record of having played at 50 consecutive All-Ireland Championships.

The Fiddler 'Round The Fairy Tree — Trad

THE CHARLADY
AN BHEAN GHLANTACHÁIN

COOKS, CLEANERS & CHILD-MINDERS

1916

STORY The term charlady can be traced back to the mid-sixteenth century. It is likely to have originated from the older terms *char* (Middle English) and *cyrr* (Old English), meaning chore or work. A charlady, or charwoman, was someone employed in domestic services such as cleaning, cooking, or child-minding. This set dance was composed in 2010 by Michael Fitzpatrick. He named it in honour of charladies he had known over the years.

In my mind, these ladies who filled multiple roles, from chambermaid, to nanny, to short order cook, were in many respects an integral part of the family. Life was good for the children of the families whose lives were touched by these ladies, because quite often the Charlady was always a reliable presence – always there with a kind word – and always there with a helping hand!

Michael Fitzpatrick, irishsetdances.net

An example of a hard working charlady was Mrs Sarah Caffrey of Dublin. She lived at 27b Corporation Buildings, near the present-day Connolly station. She worked in four family homes in the Stoneybatter and Grangegorman areas of Dublin's north inner city. Her chores over a five-day week earned her 7 shillings and 6 pence. She is remembered today as the mother of Christina Caffrey, the second youngest person to die during the Easter Rising.

The devastation of the famine, 1845-1851, had left a bitter taste and a need for change in Ireland. In 1858, the Irish Republican Brotherhood set up with similar aims to the earlier United Irishmen. They wanted to overthrow British rule and establish an independent, democratic Irish Republic. In secret, they gathered support, funding and arms for a future rebellion. In 1916, they felt the time had arrived.

On Easter Monday, 24th April 1916, The Irish Republican Brotherhood, Irish Volunteers, Irish Citizen Army and women of the Cumann na mBan* seized landmark buildings across Dublin. Patrick Pearse stood outside of the General Post Office on Sackville Street (O'Connell Street today) and read a proclamation declaring an Irish Republic. The fighting centred on the locations the rebels had captured but also spread out to surrounding areas through sniper battles.

Sarah Caffrey was standing outside her flat when sniper fighting began in the area. With baby Christina in her arms, she tried to get her children indoors to safety. As shots were fired, a stray bullet went through her hand and into Christina's back. Sarah rushed her to the North Dublin Union hospital, but to no avail. Christina died on Tuesday 25th April 1916, aged just two years old. Sarah outlived her daughter by another fifty-three years.

MUSIC & DANCE *The Charlady* was composed during the summer of 2010 by Michael Fitzpatrick. He wanted to create a new jig set dance that would be long enough to showcase a dancer's skill and stamina. He based the structure on the 8-bar step, 24-bar set found in *Kilkenny Races*. The tune was submitted for consideration to the Marie Duffy Foundation's Competition for Excellence in Irish Music Composition. It was one of two set dances added to the official list of CLRG in 2012.

6/8 time signature

8 bars in step

24 bars in set

* **Cumann na mBan**

The Irish republican women's paramilitary organisation formed to 'advance the cause of Irish liberty' and to 'assist in arming and equipping a body of Irish men for the defence of Ireland'.

The Charlady — Michael Fitzpatrick

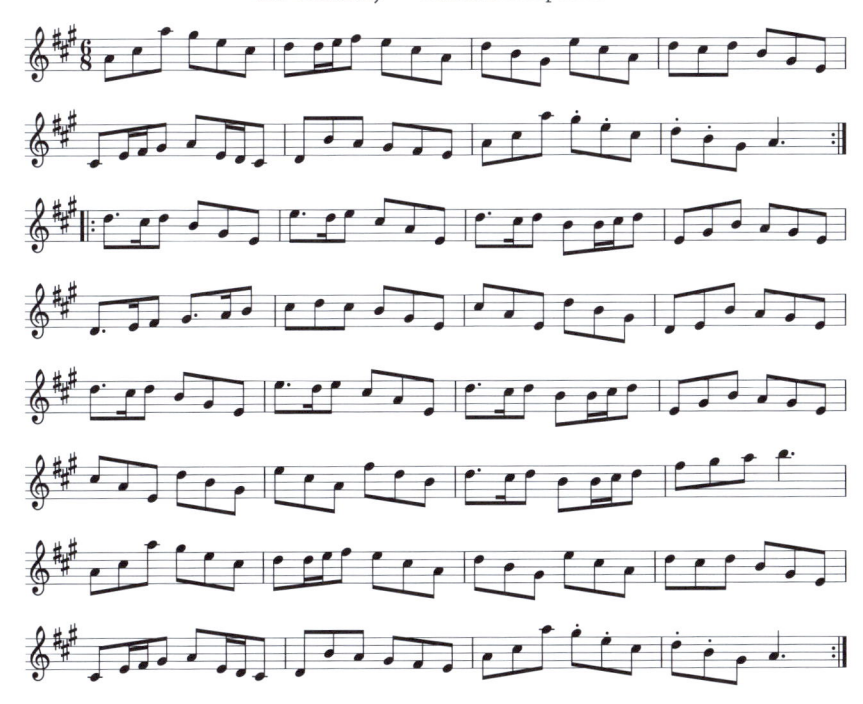

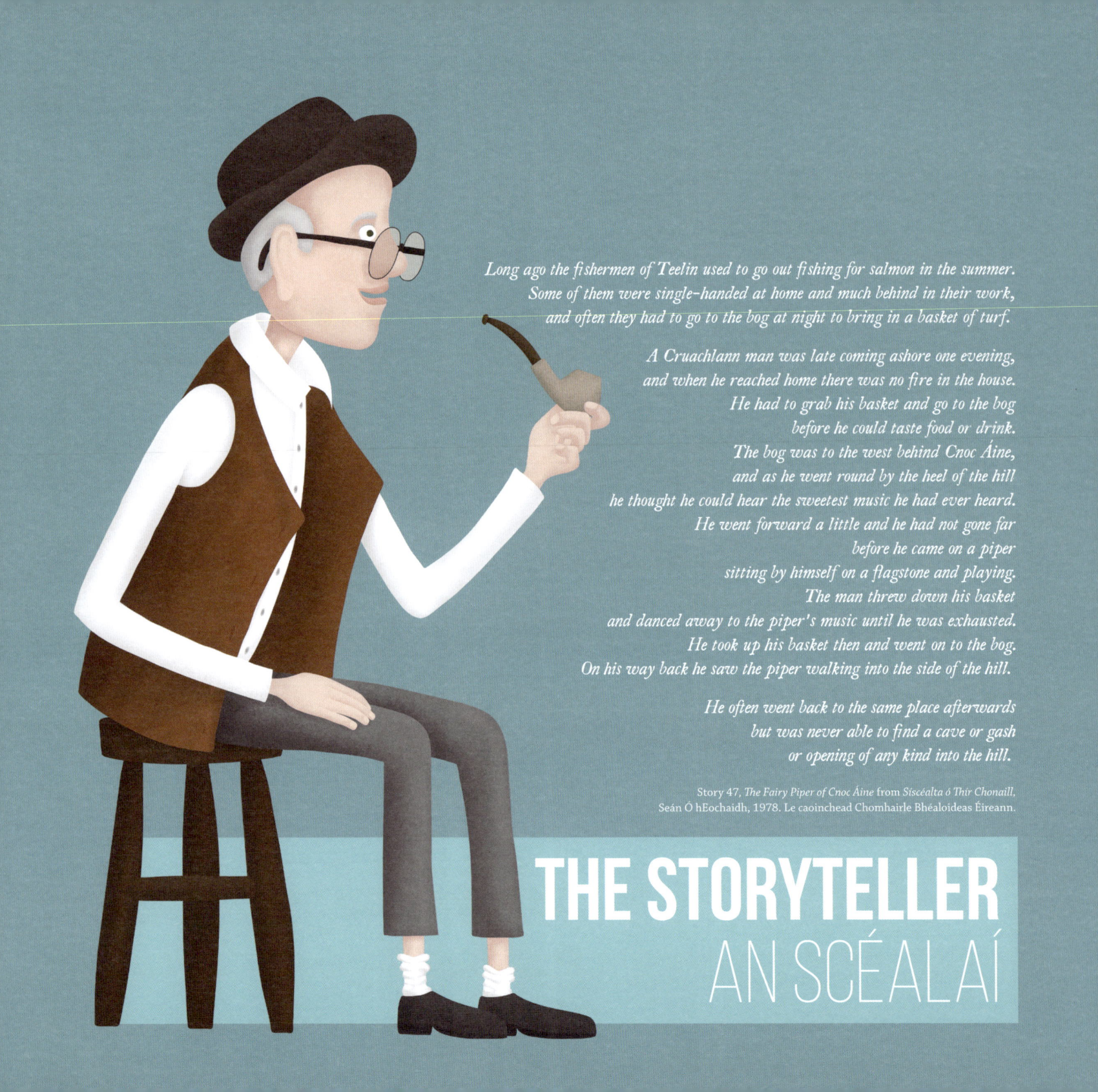

Long ago the fishermen of Teelin used to go out fishing for salmon in the summer.
Some of them were single-handed at home and much behind in their work,
and often they had to go to the bog at night to bring in a basket of turf.

A Cruachlann man was late coming ashore one evening,
and when he reached home there was no fire in the house.
He had to grab his basket and go to the bog
before he could taste food or drink.
The bog was to the west behind Cnoc Áine,
and as he went round by the heel of the hill
he thought he could hear the sweetest music he had ever heard.
He went forward a little and he had not gone far
before he came on a piper
sitting by himself on a flagstone and playing.
The man threw down his basket
and danced away to the piper's music until he was exhausted.
He took up his basket then and went on to the bog.
On his way back he saw the piper walking into the side of the hill.

He often went back to the same place afterwards
but was never able to find a cave or gash
or opening of any kind into the hill.

Story 47, *The Fairy Piper of Cnoc Áine* from *Síscéalta ó Thir Chonaill*,
Seán Ó hEochaidh, 1978. Le caoinchead Chomhairle Bhéaloideas Éireann.

THE STORYTELLER
AN SCÉALAÍ

THE SWEETEST MUSIC HE HAD EVER HEARD

1935

STORY Ireland is renowned for its oral history and folktales. Ancient Gaelic society had trained oral historians, the *file*, who memorised the history, mythology, and genealogies of the Irish. Even after the introduction of written records, legend, story, and history were still handed down through the spoken word. Storytelling by a scéalaí, seanchaí, or storyteller is a form of entertainment still practised with skill and flair today.

One such storyteller was Seán Ó hEochaidh from Donegal. In 1935, he was employed by the Irish Folklore Commission to collect the stories and fairy tales of his native Donegal. The rich wealth of material he recovered is among the last remains of the oral tradition of storytelling in the Irish language. Ó hEochaidh published these stories in *Síscéalta ó Thír Chonaill (Fairy Legends From Donegal)* in 1978. Included in the book is the story of *The Fairy Piper of Cnoc Áine*. This story was collected from Conall Ó Beirn, a fisherman from Iomaire Mhuireanáin. The English translation of the story is given on the illustration page.

In the story, a man hears beautiful pipe playing coming from behind Cnoc Áine, a hill near Teelin in Co. Donegal. He follows the music until he sees a piper sitting and playing. He is compelled to dance. Later, he sees the piper walking into the side of the hill where no cave or entrance exists.

Cnoc Áine is named after a human woman, Áine, who is said to have entered the hill to escape her violent father. Áine then became a member of the Aes Sídhe and is said to have spent her time weaving sunbeams. This links her to the Celtic goddess Áine of Cnoc Áine in Co. Limerick. The Goddess Áine is said to have wept at the funeral of harpist Thomas Connellan (see Composers, p44).

MUSIC *The Storyteller* set dance tune as danced at CLRG and An Chomhdháil competitions has a 6/8 time signature which designates it as a jig set dance. Its set and step bar structure is 8 bars for the set (A part) and 16 bars for the step (B). It is played in G major.

This matches the version composed by Don O'Doherty of Derry. It was the first set dance tune composed by O'Doherty and his family still has the original handwritten signed manuscript. O'Doherty also composed *The Four Masters* and *The Blue Eyed Rascal* set dance tunes. (see Composers, p45)

Cullinane (2016) noted some similarity between *The Storyteller* and the A part of American country song from the 1950s, *Mocking Bird Hill*. *Mocking Bird Hill* was composed by George Vaughn Norton in the 1950s. *Mocking Bird Hill* is possibly based on an earlier Swedish waltz tune called *Livet i Finnskogarna (Life in the Finland Woods)*. It was composed by Carl "Calle" Jularbo from Stockholm and recorded in 1915. The *Livet i Finnskogarna* waltz and Jularbo himself both feature in the 1947 Swedish film of the same name.

DANCE At feiseanna in Cork *The Storyteller* set dance tune was often played in waltz time (3/4) and the key of D major. This setting of *The Storyteller* set dance was arranged by Paddy Hegarty and Nellie Bergin of Cork. Their daughter, Mary Hegarty, is a well-known classical singer.

6/8
time signature

8
bars in step

16
bars in set

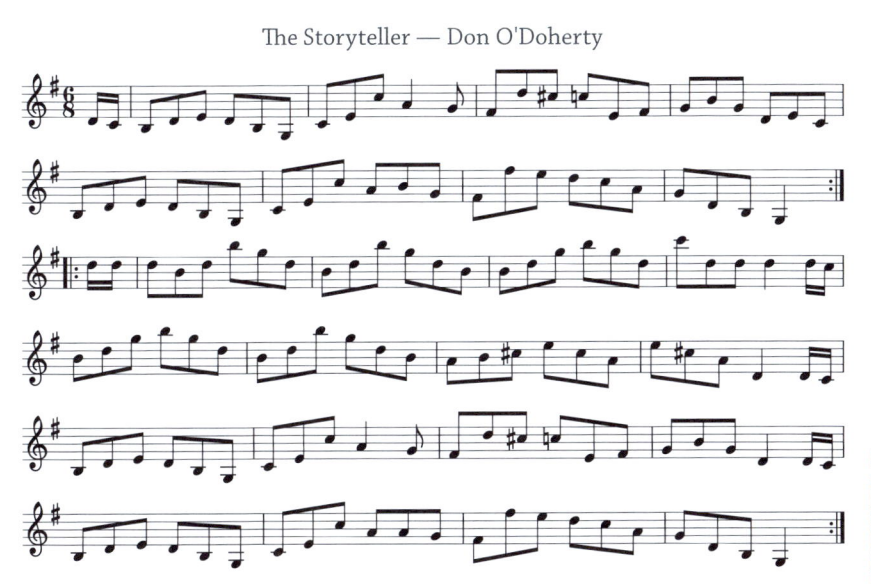

The Storyteller — Don O'Doherty

THE WHITE BLANKET
AN SÚISÍN BÁN

THE POOR CRÉATÚR

1938

STORY The illustration for *The White Blanket* is based on a folktale collected by Irish dance historian, John Cullinane. As part of his MA thesis *History of Irish Dancing in Cork 1890-1940*, 1999(a), he interviewed Bean Nic Suibhne (Mrs McSweeney) in the Cork Gaeltacht*, Múscraí. He was looking for history on the Ballyvourney setting of *The White Blanket* traditional set.

In her late nineties, Bean Nic Suibhne derived great amusement from the 'big professor from the University' not knowing the story of *An Súisín Bán*. *An Súisín Bán* translates as the white blanket or white coverlet (a quilt, or petticoat).

By Bean Nic Suibhne's telling, the 'white blanket' was the blanket of snow on the mountains during harsh Cork winters. Referring to her childhood, she recalled praying at bedtime for the snow to help insulate the 'créatúr bocht' (poor little creatures) from the freezing temperature and chill winds. These créatúr bocht were small animals like field mice, squirrels or perhaps hibernating hedgehogs**.

MUSIC The White Blanket melody has many variants and its name has many associations. The melody is found in Shields (Vol. 1, 1998) as *An Súisín Bán* (Irish for *The White Blanket*). It is also in Roche (Vol. 2, 1912) as *The Suisheen Bawn*. The Roche version is the closest to the set dance tune as it is performed today. The melody of *The White Blanket* appears in O'Neill (1903), titled there as *The White Blanket*. A tune called *Shuseen Bane*, an anglicization of *Súisín Bán*, appears in *Neal's Celebrated Irish Tunes*, 1724, but it is an unrelated melody.

SONG *The White Blanket* may be a metrical setting of the slow air and Irish language sean-nós song *Casadh an tSúgáin (The Twisting of the Hayrope)*. The song *Casadh an tSúgáin* has many versions. The version performed by the Bothy Band doesn't mention the *Súisín Bán*. The version from the Múscraí Gaeltacht has an unrelated melody but does mention the *Súisín Bán*. This version was sung by Iarla Ó Lionáid in the film *Brooklyn*, starring Saoirse Ronan.

Here is the verse that mentions the súisín bán...

Do casadh cailín deas orm in uaigneas na dtrá,
Ar lúb na coille glaise uair bheag roim lá.
Sin an fhreagar' ó a thug sí liom go ciúin agus go tláth:
"Tá an saol 'na gcoladh, bogaimís an súisín bán!"

A lovely girl met me in the loneliness of the beach.
At the bend of the green wood one hour before the day.
This was the answer she gave me quietly and gently:
"The world is asleep, let us move the white rug!"

A beautiful song in Irish from Oscar-nominated film, Brooklyn, livinglanguage.com, 2016.

DANCE In 1938, Peggy McTeggart danced a version of *The White Blanket* at the Munster Feis in Cork. She learned this setting from Cormac O'Keeffe. He got it from a dancing master named Cleaver, who taught in Cork in the mid 1800s.

McTeggart was born in 1925 in Dundalk. She taught Irish dance in Cork for over 70 years. She was a certified teacher with CLRG and was also a leading light in An Chomhdháil. She regularly performed on stage with her sisters Nancy, Betty and Maureen. Her sister, Maureen Hall, taught in numerous states in the USA. Maureen's daughters still continue the McTeggart legacy today, teaching and adjudicating throughout America.

Dr Catherine Foley has an historic setting of *The White Blanket* learned from her teacher Peggy McTeggart. Traditional versions of *The White Blanket* are acceptable in competitions run by An Chomhdháil and Cumann Rince Náisiúnta. *The White Blanket* is not designated as a traditional set for competition purposes by CLRG.

4/4 time signature

6 bars in step

12 bars in set

*****Gaeltacht**
Areas of Ireland where the language of daily life is conducted in Irish (Gaeilge). These are officially designated areas with government support for Irish language development.

******Hedgehog**
Ireland's only native hibernating animal. It is a folk belief that if hedgehogs come out of hibernation and appear on St. Bridget's day, February 1st, it will be a good spring season.

The White Blanket — Trad

THE BLUE EYED RASCAL
'RÓGAIRE NA SÚL GORMA'

I AM THE DANCE, AND THE DANCE GOES ON — 1965

STORY *The Blue Eyed Rascal* was composed by Don O'Doherty in honour of his wife Ms Mary McLaughlin ADCRG. Mary Celine McLaughlin was born in Derry in 1931. Throughout her life, she was a shining light for Irish dance in Ireland's North West. She became an acclaimed Irish dancer and established a leading dance school. Pupils of the McLaughlin School of Irish Dancing had great success in local and national competitions. In an article on Feis Muirthemine in the *Irish Press* from 1962, Patrick Lagan recounts the figure dancing competition…

But the thing that impressed me, and a packed audience, most was the brilliant figure dancing of my friends from Derry, the reigning All-Ireland and Ulster champions, the young boys and girls of the McLaughlin School. Derry was always a great place for dancing and these young people, and their teacher, are sound upholders of a good tradition. For colour and exact movement and rhythm it would have been hard to beat their presentation of "The Flight of the Earls" and "The Ring of Kerry".

Brilliant Derry dancers uphold good tradition, *Irish Press*, March 16th, 1962.

Mary was an outstanding dancing teacher, dance adjudicator, and went on to be President of An Chomhdháil*, the Congress of Irish Dance Teachers. Together with her husband Don, she was one of the organisers of the Irish dance section of Feis Dhoire Cholmcille (Derry Feis). This is the North West's premier cultural showcase for language, verse, choral competitions, drama and Irish dance. It has been running since 1922. The dance component of the Derry Feis is open platform and dancers from both An Chomhdháil and CLRG are welcome to participate.

Many of Mary's pupils went on to sit the dance teacher exams and establish their own dancing school. Mary's niece, Orlaith Leppard, also became a dance teacher and continues Mary's legacy as teacher of the McLaughlin School. Mary took her passion for Irish dance with her to the next life when she passed on the 23rd of January 2007.

The inscription on her memorial includes 'Rógaire na Súl Gorma', The Blue Eyed Rascal, and an excerpt from the hymn *Lord of the Dance*…

*They buried my body and they thought I'd gone,
But I am the Dance, and the Dance goes on.*
Mary McLaughlin, RIP.

MUSIC *The Blue Eyed Rascal*, composed by Don O'Donerty, was published in 1965 in *A Collection of the Dance Music of Ireland* compiled by Pat McNulty. Don O'Doherty also composed *The Storyteller* and *The Four Masters* set dances. (see Composers, p45). In 1978, there was a query in *Céim*, the CLRG publication, as to why *The Blue Eyes Rascall* was not amongst the set dances permitted in CLRG. The comment from the editor was as follows…

*Not being a traditional tune,
it is unlikely to find a place on the official list.*
Céim, Vol. 32, 1978.

Ironically, the set dance was added to the official list in 2004 and is now extremely popular at CLRG events.

DANCE American Irish dancing teacher and adjudicator Russell Beaton recalls learning a version of the step of *The Blue Eyed Rascal* from Mary McLaughlin ADCRG. Beaton also had the good fortune to be accompanied by Mary's husband, Don O'Doherty, the composer of the tune.

The Blue Eyed Rascal — Don O'Doherty

4/4 time signature

8 bars in step

12 bars in set

*****An Chomhdháil**
An Chomhdháil, otherwise referred to as The Congress of Irish Dance Teachers has been in existence officially since 1970, following a split from CLRG in the late 1960s.

THE WANDERING MUSICIAN
AN CEOLTÓIR FÁNACH

AT HOME AND AWAY

1985

MUSIC In 1985, the All-Ireland of An Chomhdháil was held in Cork City Hall. A music competition was organised, inviting the composition of new set dance tunes which musicians were requested to submit and play.

Phelim Warren, a piano accordion player from Dublin, composed *The Wandering Musician* and entered the competition. The event was adjudicated by Professor Micheál Ó Súilleabháin, a composer of note and then lecturer in music at University College Cork. Phelim got second place, and *The Wandering Musician* became a set dance of An Chomhdháil.

STORY Although the title, *The Wandering Musician*, could reference any well-travelled musician, Phelim named it in reference to his own travels. Phelim and his brother Kevin were both frequent musicians at feiseanna and festivals nationwide and abroad.

Phelim is also an avid football fan and supporter of the Irish national team. He has followed the 'Boys in Green' to away games across the world. He is well-known for bringing his accordion with him to lead the supporters' sing-song before and after games. A few years after composing *The Wandering Musician*, Phelim and friends travelled to Italy for the Italia '90 football World Cup. Ireland drew 1-1 against Holland in Palermo. With his accordion in hand, Phelim led the singing of thousands of Irish supporters at the after-party in Terrasini.

Furthering the family's music tradition, Kevin Warren and his son Seán are acclaimed dance accompanists. They regularly perform throughout Ireland and record under the label of The Wandering Musicians. Seán also performs on cello in the contemporary traditional band, Strung. Strung have performed across the UK and Ireland, and recently in Paris.

Being a wandering musician is a familiar concept to many Irish traditional musicians. There is a long heritage of musicians travelling the country, going back to the Gaelic bards and blind harpers. In more recent centuries, Traveller musicians have played a central role in the transmission of musical repertoire from one area of the country to another.

The Dunne Brothers, Joseph, Michael and Christy were highly respected Traveller musicians who wandered throughout the country during the 1940s, 50s and 60s. The Dunne Brothers' nephew, Mickey Dunne, is a well-known uilleann pipe player and pipe maker from Limerick. Mickey's daughter, Niamh Dunne, is a member of the contemporary traditional music group, Beoga. Through Beoga, Niamh is another well-travelled wandering musician, playing at concerts and festivals across the world. Beoga collaborated on two songs with Ed Sheeran, *Galway Girl* and *Nancy Mulligan*, and have toured with him.

DANCE *The Wandering Musician* set dance has a close connection between composer and choreographer. Phelim Warren's mother is Brenda Bastable, a well-known Irish dancing teacher of Scoil Rince Bastable Warren based in Dublin. She choreographed a setting of *The Wandering Musician* for Phelim's brother, Kevin Warren, to perform at feiseanna later that year. This set dance is regularly danced at both An Chomhdháil and CLRG feiseanna today.

6/8 time signature

8 bars in step

16 bars in set

The Wandering Musician — Phelim Warren

REFERENCES

Asterisk denotes texts referenced directly within the text

A Treasury of Irish Folklore. (1967). New York: Crown.

Aird, J. and Johnson, J. (1786). *A selection of Scotch, English, Irish, and foreign airs. Adapted for the fife, violin, or German flute. Vol. II*. Glasgow: Jas. Aird.

*Aird, J. and Johnson, J. (1795). *A selection of Scotch, English, Irish, and foreign airs. Vol. III*. Glasgow: Jas. Aird.

*Akenson, D. (1986). *The Orangeman: The Life & Times of Ogle Gowan*. Toronto [Ont.]: Lorimer.

*Atkins, M. (2008). *The Beggar's 'Children'*. Cambridge Scholars Publishing.

Bateman, J. and Bell, J. (1865). *The excise officer's manual*. London: W. Maxwell.

Bayor, R. and Meagher, T. (1996). *The New York Irish*. Baltimore: Johns Hopkins University Press.

Bennett, G. (2017). *History of Bandon, and the principal towns in the west riding of Co. Cork*. [S.l.]: Forgotten Books.

Boullier, D. (1998). *Exploring Irish music and dance*. Dublin: O'Brien.

Breathnach, B. (1963). *Ceol Rince na h-Éireann 1*. Baile Átha Cliath: Oifig an tSoláthair.

Breathnach, B. (1976). *Ceol Rince na h-Éireann 2*. Baile Átha Cliath: Offing an tSoláthair.

Breathnach, B. (1977). *Folk Music and dances of Ireland. Rev.Ed*. Mercier Press.

Breathnach, B. (1983). *Dancing in Ireland*. Miltown-Malbay, Co. Clare: Dal gCais Publications in association with the Folklore and Folk Music Society of Clare.

Breathnach, B. (1985). *Ceol Rince na h-Éireann 3*. Baile Átha Cliath: An Gúm.

Breathnach, B. (1991). *Ceol Rince na h-Éireann 1*. 2nd ed. Dublin: An Gúm.

Breathnach, B. and Small, J. (1996). *Ceol Rince na h-Éireann 4*. Baile Átha Cliath: An Gúm.

Breathnach, B. and Small, J. (1999). *Ceol Rince na h-Éireann 5*. Bailey Atha Cliath: An Gúm.

Brewer, J. (2015). *Beauties of Ireland* [S.l.]: Forgotten Books.

Bunting, E. and O'Sullivan, D. (1967). *Bunting collection of Irish folk music and songs*. London.

*Bunting, E. (1796). *A general collection of the ancient music of Ireland*. London: Printed & sold for the editor by Clementi.

Carleton, W. (1873). *Tales and stories of the Irish peasantry*. New York: D. & J. Sadlier.

Carleton, W. and Hurley, J. (2001). *Irish gangs and stick-fighting*. [Philadelphia]: Xlibris.

Carolan, T. and Ó Máille, T. (1916). *Amhráin Cearbhalláin*. London: The Irish Texts Society.

Carolan, T. and Rowsome, C. (2011). *The complete Carolan songs & airs*. Dublin: Waltons Publishing.

Carson, C. (1998). *Last night's fun*. New York: North Point Press.

Chamier, F. (1837). The naval history of Great Britain. London: R. Bentley.

Chappell, W. and Macfarren, G. (1871). *The Ballad Literature and Popular Music of the Olden Time, etc*. Chappell & Co.: London.

Clark, W. (1955). *The early Irish stage*. Oxford: Clarendon.

Clerk, J. (1827). *An essay on naval tactics, by John Clerk*. Adam Black, Edinburgh.

Cooke (1795). *Cooke's selection of Twenty One Favorite Original Irish Airs*.

Colum, P. (1967). A treasury of Irish folklore. New York: Crown.

Cox, W. (1996). Wolfe Tone: An Address To the People of Ireland on the Present Important Crisis.. Belfast: Athol Books.

*Crosby, B. (1808). *The Irish Musical Repository*. London: Printed for B. Crosby & Co.

Cuchulainn, Hull, E. and Reid, S. (1909). *Cuchulainn, the Hound of Ulster. By Eleanor Hull … With sixteen illustrations in colour by Stephen Reid*. George G. Harrap & Co.: London.

*Cullinane, J. (1999). *Aspects of the history of Irish dancing in Ireland, England, New Zealand, North America and Australia*. Cork: J.P. Cullinane.

Cullinane, J. (n.d.). Set Dances. Unpublished Article.

Cullinane, J. (1999). *Irish dancing costumes*. Cork: John P. Cullinane.

Cullinane, J. (2001). *Further aspects of the history of Irish dancing in Ireland, Scotland, Canada, America, New Zealand and Australia*. Cork: John Cullinane.

Cullinane, J. (2003). *An Coimisiún le Rincí Gaelacha (Irish Dancing Commission)*. Cork City, Ireland: John Cullinane.

*Cullinane, J. (2017). *Aspects of the history of Irish dancing in Dublin 1890-2017*. Cork City, Ireland: J. Cullinane.

*Cullinane, J. (1999(a)). *History of Irish Dancing in Cork 1890 -1940.*. MA. UCC.

*de Grae, Paul (2017). *O'Neill Source Notes*. Unpublished.

Dolan, T. (1999). *A dictionary of Hiberno-English*. Dublin: Gill & Macmillan.

Donaldson, W. (1988). The Jacobite Song: political myth and national identity. Aberdeen: Aberdeen University Press.

Drennan, W., McTier, M., Agnew, J. and Luddy, M. (1998). The Drennan-McTier letters. Dublin: Women's History Project in association with the Irish Manuscripts Commission.

Duffy, S. ed., (2005). *Mediaeval Ireland, An Encyclopaedia*. New York: Routledge.

Duffy, J. (2015). Children of the Rising. Hachette Books.

Eliot, G. (2016). *The mill on the Floss*. New York: Open Road Integrated Media.

*Fleischmann, A. (1998). *Sources of Irish traditional music, c. 1600-1855*. New York: Garland.

Foley, C. (2001). Perceptions of Irish Step Dance: National, Global, and Local. *Dance Research Journal*, 33(1), p.34.

*Foley, C. (2013). *Step dancing in Ireland: culture and history*. London: Ashgate.

Fraser, E. and Wellington, A. (1913). *The Soldiers whom Wellington led. Deeds of daring, chivalry and renown ... With twelve illustrations and five maps*. Methuen & Co.: London.

Gibbons, S. (2004). Captain Rock, night errant. Dublin: Four Courts Press.

Glen, J. (1900). Early Scottish Melodies. Edinburgh: J&R Glen.

Gow, N. (1795). *A third collection of Strathspey reels &c. for the piano-forte*. Edinr.: Printed & sold by N. & M. Stewart.

Grattan Flood, W. (1906). *A History of Irish music by Wm. H. Grattan Flood*. Dublin: Browne & Nolan.

* Grattan-Flood, W. (1911). *The story of the bagpipe*. London: Scott.

Groeger, K. (2016). *Little Book of Youghal*. The History Press.

Gwyn, R. (2007). John A. The man who made us. [Toronto]: Random House Canada.

Hall, F. (2008). *Competitive Irish dance*. Madison (Wis.): Macater.

Hall, S. (2016). *Ireland, Its scenery ,character and history,*. [S.l.]: Forgotten Books.

Hardy, T. (2018). *Far From the Madding Crowd*. La Vergne: Dreamscape Media.

Harkin, M. (2013). *Inishowen, Its history,Traditions and Antiquities*. [S.l.]: Lulu Press Inc.

Hast, D. and Scott, S. (2011). Music in Ireland. New York [u.a.]: Oxford Univ. Press.

* Hickey, D. (1999). *Stone Mad for Music*. Dublin: Marino.

Hogg, J. (1819). *The Jacobite relics of Scotland ; the songs, airs, and legends, of the adherents to the House of Stuart.*. Edinburgh: Printed for William Blackwood.

Hook, H. (2010). *Empires of the Imagination: Politics, War, and the Arts in the British World, 1750-1850*. London: Profile Books Ltd.

Hopkins, F. (2003). Rare old Dublin. Douglas Village, Cork: Marino.

Howe, E. (1865). Songs of Ireland: containing about 175 of the gems of Hibernia's songs

Journal of the Irish Folk Song Society. (1967). London usw.: Dawson & Sons.

* Joyce, P. (1873). *Ancient Irish music, comprising 100 airs hitherto unpublished*. Dublin: McGlashan and Gill.

Joyce, P. (1912). *Ancient Irish music*. Dublin: M.H. Gill & Sons.

Joyce, P. (2016). *Old Irish Folk Music and songs*. [S.l.]: Forgotten Books.

Joyce, P., Nunan, P. and Sullivan, A. (1900). *Atlas and cyclopedia of Ireland*. New York:

Kay, P. (1995). *A Jacobite legacy*. Loughborough: Soar Valley Music.

Kidson, F. and Neal, M. (2012). English folk-song and dance. Cambridge: Cambridge University Press.

* Kohl, J. (1844). *Travels in Ireland*. London: Bruce and Wyld

* Le Fanu, W. R. (1893). *Seventy Years of Irish Life: being anecdotes and reminiscences*. London: E. Arnold.

Lee, J. (1791). *John Lee's Collection of Country Dances for the present year 1791*. Dublin.

Leerssen, J. (1986). *Mere Irish & fíor-ghael*. Amsterdam: John Benjamins Pub. Co.

Lenman, B. (1980). *The Jacobite risings in Britain, 1689-1746*. London: Eyre Methuen.

Livery, B. (2007). *Shield of Empire - The Royal Navy and Scotland.*. Edinburgh: Berlin Limited.

* Mac Coitir, N. (2015). *Ireland's birds*. [S.l.]: The Collins Press.

Mac Coitir, N. and D'Arcy, G. (2010). *Ireland's animals*. Collins Press.

MacCafferty, J. (2007). *The Deep Green Pool*. Derry [Ireland]: Guildhall Press.

Máille, T. (2016). *Ámhráin Chearbhalláin*. [S.l.]: Forgotten Books.

Marsh, C. (2013). *Music and society in early modern England*. Cambridge: Cambridge University Press.

Maye, B. (2016). An Irishman's Diary on the debt we owe to George Petrie, the 'father of Irish archaeology. *The Irish Times*.

Mc Aulay, K. (2016). *Our Ancient National Airs: Scottish Song Collecting from the Enlightenment to the Romantic Era.*. New York: Routledge.

* Mc Nulty, P. (1965). *A Collection of the Dance Music of Ireland*.

McCullough, L. and McCullough, L. (n.d.). *What whistle would you play at your mother's funeral?*

McDonnell, J. and Devine, F. (2008). *Songs of struggle and protest*. Dublin: Irish Labour History Society.

* McGowan, J. and McGloin, A. (2015). *Sligo Folk Tales*.

McNeill, W. (1949). The Introduction of the Potato into Ireland. *The Journal of Modern History*, 21(3), pp.218-222.

Moloney, C. and Carolan, N. (2000). *The Irish music manuscripts of Edward Bunting (1773-1843)*. Dublin: Irish Traditional Music Archive - Taisce Cheol Dúchais Éireann.

Moylan, T. ed., (2000). *The Age of Revolution in the Irish Song Tradition, 1776 to 1815.*. Dublin: The Lilliput Press Ltd.

Murphy, G. (1956). *Early Irish Lyrics, eighth to twelfth century. Edited with translation, notes, and glossary by G. Murphy*. Clarendon Press: Oxford.

Murphy, G. (1970). Early Irish lyrics. Oxford: Clarendon Press.

* Ni Bhriain, O. (2010). *An examination of the creative process in competitive Irish step dance*. Ph.D. University of Limerick.

Ní Bhriain, O. (2008). *The terminology of Irish dance*. Madison, Wis.: Macater.

Ni Shéaghdha, N. (1985). *Collectors of Irish Manuscripts: Motives and Methods*.

Ó h-Allmhuráin, G. (2008). *O'Brien pocket history of Irish traditional music*. Dublin: O'Brien.

Ó hEidhin, M. (1975). *Cas Amhrán*. Indreabhán: Cló Iar-Chonnachta.

Ó hEochaidh, S., Mac Néill, M. and Ó Catháin, S. (1977). *Fairy legends from Donegal =*. Dublin: Comhairle Bhéaloideas Éireann.

Ó Canainn, T. (1978). *Traditional music in Ireland*. London: Routledge & Kegan Paul.

O'Connor, M. (2010). *Poems, pastorals, and dialogues. ... by Morgan O'Conner*. [Place of publication not identified]: Gale Ecco, Print Editions.

* O'Farrell, P. (1804). *O'Farrell's collection of national Irish music for the union pipes, comprising a variety of the most favorite slow & sprightly tunes, set in proper stile (sic) & taste, with variations and adapted likewise for the German flute, violin, flagelet, piano, & harp, with a selection of favorite Scotch tunes, also a treatise with the most perfect instructions ever yet published for the pipes*.

O'G. (1833). Sir Walter Raleigh's House at Youghal. *The Dublin Penny Journal*, 1(48), p.377.

* O'Keefe, J. and O' Brien, A. (1902). *A handbook of Irish dances: with an essay on their origin and history*. Dublin: O'Donoghue & Co.

O'Loughlin, T. (1999). *St. Patrick*. London: Triangle.

O'Mahony, J. (1903). *The Sunny Side of Ireland ... With seven maps and over 160 illustrations, and a chapter on the natural history of the South and West of Ireland, by R. Lloyd Praeger. (Second edition, rewritten and enlarged.)*. Dublin: Alex. Thom & Co.

* O'Neill, F. (1903). *Music of Ireland*. Chicago.

* O'Neill, F. (1907). *Dance Music of Ireland (1001 Gems)..* Chicago.

* O'Neill, F. (1910). *Irish folk music*. Chicago: The Regan Printing House.

* O'Neill, F. (1913). *Irish minstrels and musicians*. Chicago, Ill: Regan.

* O'Neill, F. (1922). *Waifs and strays of Gaelic melody*. Chicago.

O'Shea, H. (2010). *The making of Irish traditional music*. Cork: Cork University Press.

O Súilleabháin, M. (1987). *Innovation and Tradition in the music of Tommy Potts*. Queen's University Belfast.

* O'Sullivan, D. (1958). *Carolan - The Life Times and Music of an Irish Harper*. London: Rutledge and K. Paul.

O' Sullivan, J. (n.d.). *Eoghan Rua Ó Súilleabháin- in his time and Places*.

* Oswald, J. (1750). *The Caledonian Pocket Companion containing a favourite collection of Scots tunes*. London: I. Oswald.

* Parry, J. (1781). *British Harmony, Being a Collection of Ancient Welsh Airs*. London: John Parry.

Petrie, G. (1855). *Petrie (George) LL. D., M.R.I.A. The Petrie Collection of the Ancient Music of Ireland. Arranged for the pianoforte. Edited by G. Petrie. Vol. I. [and pp. 1-48 of vol. II.]*. Dublin.

* Petrie, G. and Stanford, C. (1902). *The complete collection of Irish music*. London: Published for the Irish Literary Society of London by Boosey.

Petrie, G., Cooper, D. and Ó Laoire, L. (2002). *The Petrie Collection of the ancient music of Ireland*. Cork: Cork University Press.

* Phelan, S. (2014). *Dance in Ireland*. Newcastle upon Tyne: Cambridge Scholars Publishing.

Price, G. and Owen, M. (1987). *Ireland and the Celtic connection*. Gerrards Cross: Smythe.

Quinn, T. (1997). *Irish dancing*. Glasgow: Harper Collins Publishers.

Ralls-Mac Leod, K. (2000). *Music and the Celtic otherworld*. New York: St. Martin's Press.

* Riley, E. (1817). *Riley's Flute Melodies. Vol. II*. New-York: Engraved, printed and sold by the editor, no. 29 Chatham-Street.

Robb, M. (1998). *Irish dancing costume*. Dublin: Country House.

* Roche, F. (1912). *Collection of Irish airs, marches and dance tunes*. Dublin [etc.].

* Roche, F. (1927). *Collection of Irish Airs, Marches and Dance Tunes, Vol. III,*. 1st ed.

Roche, F. (1982). *The Roche collection of traditional Irish music*. New York: Oak Publications.

Senior, H. (1972). Gowan, Ogle Robert. Dictionary of Canadian Biography University of Toronto/Université Laval.

Sheehan, J. J. (1902). *A Guide to Irish Dancing*. London: John Denvir.

* Shields, H. (1998). *Tunes of the Munster pipers. Vol. I*. Dublin: Irish Traditional Music Archive.

* Shields, H. and Shields, L. (2013). *Tunes of the Munster Pipers Vol. II*. Dublin: Irish Traditional Music Archive.

Shiels, D. (2013). *Stories of the Irish in the American Civil War*. Stroud: History.

Smith, T. (2012). *Ancestral imprints*. Cork: Cork University Press.

* Stevenson, J. and Ward, S. (1807). *A selection of Irish melodies, with symphonies and accompaniments*. London: Printed & sold at J. Power's Music & Instrument Ware House.

Storey, R. (2005). *Irish dancing*. London: Franklin Watts.

Strachan, J. and Nally, C. (2012). *Advertising, Literature and Print Culture in Ireland, 1891-1922.*. Palgrave Macmillan.

The Irish Times. (2018). *Rake's progress – An Irishman's Diary on the life, loves and wagers of Thomas 'Buck' Whaley*. [online] Available at: https://www.irishtimes.com/opinion/rake-s-progress-an-irishman-s-diary-on-the-life-loves-and-wagers-of-thomas-buck-whaley-1.2902967 [Accessed 15 Feb. 2018].

The standard Orange song book. (1848). Armagh: Printed at the Armagh Guardian Office.

* Thomas, J. (1862). *Welsh Melodies*. London.

Thompson, E. (1999). *Who was Saint Patrick?* Woodbridge: Boydell.

* *Thompson's compleat collection of 200 favourite country dances*. (1770). London: Printed for Charles and Samuel Thompsons, in St Pauls Church Yard where may be had the yearly dances & minuets.

Thomson, M. (1822). *Thomson's Collection of the Songs of Burns, Sir Walter Scott et al,*. London: Preston.

Tubridy, M. (1998). *A selection of Irish traditional step dances*. Dublin: Brooks Academy.

* *Twenty Four New Country Dances for the Year 1780*. (1780). London: Printed for T. Skillern.

Vallely, F. (2011). *The companion to Irish traditional music*. Cork: Cork University Press.

* *Vocal music, or, The songster's companion*. (1772). [London]: Printed for J. Bew.

Wagner, G. (2018). *Miss Palmer's Diar : The Secret Journals of a Victorian Lady*. I. B. Tauris & Company, Limited.

Ward, F. (2016). *Processes of transmission in Irish traditional music: approaching a virtual orality*. Ph.D. University of Limerick.

* Wentz, E.W. (1909). *The Fairy-faith in Celtic countries, its psychical origin and nature*. Rennes: Impr. de Oberthur.

* Whelan, F. (2007). *The complete guide to Irish dance*. Belfast: Appletree Press.

Wilde, W. (2015). *Lough Corrib*. [S.l.]: Forgotten Books.

Williams, S. (2010). *Focus: Irish traditional music*. New York: Routledge.

Wulff, H. (2009). *Dancing at the crossroads*. New York [u.a.]: Berghahn Books.

ONLINE SOURCES

Comhaltas Globally Promotes Traditional Irish Music Dance Culture for Students, Educators, Visitors, Musicians & Journalists. [online] Comhaltas.ie. Available at: https://comhaltas.ie/ [Accessed 2 Jun. 2018].

1066.co.nz. (2018). List of High Kings of Ireland. [online] Available at: http://www.1066.co.nz/Mosaic%20DVD/whoswho/text/List_of_High_Kings_of_Ireland[1]htm [Accessed 6 May 2018].

An Sionnach Fionn. (2018). An Sí. [online] Available at: https://ansionnachfionn.com/seanchas-mythology/an-si/ [Accessed 6 May 2018].

An Sionnach Fionn. (2018). Tuatha Dé Danann. [online] Available at: https://ansionnachfionn.com/seanchas-mythology/tuatha-de-danann/ [Accessed 6 May 2018].

Anon, (2018). [online] Available at: https://www.museum.ie/The-Collections/Documentation-Discoveries/July-2014/Medieval-Irish-Mether [Accessed 17 Feb. 2018].

Araltas.com. (2015). O'Donnell coat of arms and Family History. [online] Available at: http://www.araltas.com/features/odonnell/ [Accessed 8 Feb. 2015].

Archive.org. (2018). Select documents illustrating the history of trade unionism. 1. The tailoring trade;. [online] Available at: http://www.archive.org/stream/selectdocumentsi00galtiala#page/66/mode/2up [Accessed 10 Mar. 2016].

Askaboutireland.ie. (2018). Dease: A Complete History of the Westmeath Hunt. [online] Available at: http://www.askaboutireland.ie/reading-room/digital-book-collection/digital-books-by-county/westmeath/dease-a-complete-history-/ [Accessed 15 Feb. 2018].

Ballads.bodleian.ox.ac.uk. (2018). Viewing: Harding B 25(1641). [online] Available at: http://ballads.bodleian.ox.ac.uk/view/sheet/11113 [Accessed 15 Feb. 2018].

Ballinagree.freeservers.com. (2018). Pádraig Ó Miléadha (1877 – 1947): Poet of Ireland and of Wales. [online] Available at: http://www.ballinagree.freeservers.com/mileadha.html [Accessed 6 May 2018].

Ballymoteheritage.com. (2018). Cite a Website - Cite This For Me. [online] Available at: http://ballymoteheritage.com/wp-content/uploads/2016/07/41-2008.pdf [Accessed 17 Feb. 2018].

bbc.co.uk. (2018). Your Place And Mine - Topics - War - WW2 - Poem for a fallen brother. [online] Available at: http://www.bbc.co.uk/northernireland/yourplaceandmine/topics/your_questions/Anew04079.shtml [Accessed 15 Feb. 2018].

Belfastforum.co.uk. (2018). ITL Cafeys Irish Temperance League. [online] Available at: http://www.belfastforum.co.uk/index.php?topic=32231.0 [Accessed 15 Feb. 2018].

Billhaneman.ie. (2018). [online] Available at: http://billhaneman.ie/IMM/IMM-XIX.html [Accessed 15 Feb. 2018].

Billhaneman.ie. (2018). [online] Available at: http://billhaneman.ie/IMM/IMM-XXXI.html [Accessed 17 Feb. 2018].

Celt.ucc.ie. (2018). Annals of the Four Masters. [online] Available at: https://celt.ucc.ie/published/T100005A [Accessed 6 May 2018].

Clrg.ie. (2018). An Coimisiún Le Rincí Gaelacha | The Irish Dancing Commission. [online] Available at: https://www.clrg.ie/index.php/en/ [Accessed 2 Jun. 2018].

Confessio.ie. (2018). 'My name is Patrick... | St. Patrick's Confessio. [online] Available at: https://confessio.ie/ [Accessed 6 May 2018].

Corofin.galway-ireland.ie. (2018). Knockma Galway Knockma Hill Galway Queen Maeve Finvarra Ireland. [online] Available at: http://corofin.galway-ireland.ie/knockma.htm [Accessed 15 Feb. 2018].

Crn.ie. (2018). Cumann Rince Naisiunta. [online] Available at: http://www.crn.ie/ [Accessed

Derryjournal.com. (2018). Don O'Doherty - his memory will live on. [online] Available at: https://www.derryjournal.com/news/don-o-doherty-his-memory-will-live-on-1-2125708 [Accessed 15 Feb. 2018].

Doegen.ie. (2018). An táilliúir aerach - Mánus Ó Creag | The Doegen Records Web Project. [online] Available at: https://www.doegen.ie/LA_1263d2 [Accessed 7 Aug. 2015].

Encyclopedia Britannica. (2018). Battle of the Saintes | Summary. [online] Available at: https://www.britannica.com/event/Battle-of-the-Saintes [Accessed 15 Feb. 2018].

Eprints.maynoothuniversity.ie. (2018). Cite a Website - Cite This For Me. [online] Available at: http://eprints.maynoothuniversity.ie/4738/1/Final%20version%20of%20thesis.pdf [Accessed 17 Feb. 2018].

FarmIreland.ie. (2018). Chris Ryan: Born and bred to lead the Scarteens - FarmIreland.ie. [online] Available at: https://www.independent.ie/business/farming/chris-ryan-born-and-bred-to-lead-the-scarteens-30340871.html [Accessed 15 Feb. 2018].

Festival Dance Teachers Association. (2018). Festival Dance Teachers Association. [online] Available at: http://www.fdta.net/ [Accessed 2 Jun. 2018].

Fightland. (2018). Real Irish Fighting: A History of Shillelagh Law and Hob-Nailed Boot Stomping | Fightland. [online] Available at: http://fightland.vice.com/blog/real-irish-fighting-a-history-of-shillelagh-law-and-hob-nailed-boot-stomping [Accessed 17 Feb. 2018]..

Getty Images. (2018). An engraving from Shakespeare's 'The Winter's Tale' showing a scene.... [online] Available at: https://www.gettyimages.co.uk/license/507531728 [Accessed 15 Feb. 2018].

Group, D. (2018). O'Rourkes Noble Feast. [online] Dromahair Heritage. Available at: https://dromahairheritage.wordpress.com/2017/03/08/orourkes-noble-feast/ [Accessed 17 Feb. 2018].

hÉireann, S. and hÉireann, S. (2018). 1636 – The Annals of the Four Masters is completed.. [online] Stair na hÉireann/History of Ireland. Available at: https://stairnaheireann.net/2016/08/10/1636-the-annals-of-the-four-masters-is-completed-2/ [Accessed 15 Feb. 2018].

Hill, C. (2018). The English Revolution 1640 by Christopher Hill. [online] Marxists.org. Available at: https://www.marxists.org/archive/hill-christopher/english-revolution/ [Accessed 15 Feb. 2018].

Historic UK. (2018). The Battle of Culloden, 1746. [online] Available at: http://www.historic-uk.com/HistoryMagazine/DestinationsUK/The-Battle-of-Culloden/ [Accessed 15 Feb. 2018].

History Ireland. (2018). Clock Gate, Youghal, Co. Cork. [online] Available at: http://www.historyireland.com/early-modern-history-1500-1700/clock-gate-youghal-co-cork/ [Accessed 15 Feb. 2018].

History Ireland. (2018). The Introduction of the Potato into Ireland. [online] Available at: http://www.historyireland.com/early-modern-history-1500-1700/the-introduction-of-the-potato-into-ireland/ [Accessed 15 Feb. 2018].

http://dtic.mil/dtic/tr/fulltext/u2/a288841.pdf. (n.d.).

http://www.yorku.ca/inpar/colloquy_ogrady.pdf p128. (2018).

Hull, E. (2018). A History of Ireland and Her People. [online] Libraryireland.com. Available at: http://www.libraryireland.com/HullHistory/Contents.php [Accessed 6 May 2018].

Ibiblio.org. (2018). The Fiddler's Companion. [online] Available at: http://www.ibiblio.org/fiddlers/ [Accessed 2 Jun. 2018].

II, E., Shakespeare, W., William, P., Obama, B., Charles, P., Monroe, M., Philip, P., Mandela, N. and Chaplin, C. (2018). Le César de 1815 (Napoleon as Caesar of 1815), 1815. Artist: Anonymous. [online] Getty Images. Available at: https://www.gettyimages.ie/detail/news-photo/le-c%C3%A9sar-de-1815-1815-found-in-the-collection-of-the-state-news-photo/464440757#le-csar-de-1815-1815-found-in-the-collection-of-the-state-borodino-picture-id464440757 [Accessed 15 Feb. 2018].

Independent.ie. (2018). Women in the nation's capital struggled to survive – even before the Rising - Independent.ie. [online] Available at: https://www.independent.ie/irish-news/1916/rising-perspectives/women-in-the-nations-capital-struggled-to-survive-even-before-the-rising-31126023.html [Accessed 17 Feb. 2018].

Irish Family History Centre. (2018). Stoking Bram's imagination - stories from Irish history. [online] Available at: https://www.irishfamilyhistorycentre.com/article/stoking-brams-imagination-stories-from-irish-history [Accessed 17 Feb. 2018].

Irish Walled Towns Network. (2018). History of Youghal. [online] Available at: http://irishwalledtownsnetwork.ie/page/youghal/youghal-info [Accessed 15 Feb. 2018].

Irishcultureandcustoms.com. (2018). Shillelagh Blackthorn Walking Stick - World Cultures European. [online] Available at: http://www.irishcultureandcustoms.com/AEmblem/Shillelagh.html [Accessed 7 Jan. 2018].

Irishfables.com. (2018). Brehon law | The Lost Tales of Fionn Mac Cumhaill. [online] Available at: https://irishfables.com/tag/brehon-law/ [Accessed 17 Feb. 2018].

Irishpage.com. (2018). 180 Máire Brún - Mary Browne. [online] Available at: http://www.irishpage.com/songs/carolan/browne.htm [Accessed 17 Feb. 2018].

Irishpage.com. (2018). 199 Pléaráca na Ruarcach - O'Rourke's Feast. [online] Available at: http://www.irishpage.com/songs/carolan/feast.htm [Accessed 6 May 2018].

Irishtemperanceleague.com. (2018). Cite a Website - Cite This For Me. [online] Available at: http://irishtemperanceleague.com/downloads/ITL%20EXECUTIVE%20SUMMARY.pdf [Accessed 15 Feb. 2018].

ITMA. (2017). The journeyman tailor, song / Eddie Butcher, singing in English | ITMA. [online] Available at: https://www.itma.ie/digital-library/sound/journeyman_tailor_eddie_butcher [Accessed 17 Feb. 2017].

ITMA. (2018). Features | ITMA. [online] Available at: https://www.itma.ie/features/notated-collections/roche_vol-2_296-354 [Accessed 2 Jun. 2018].

Itma.ie. (2018). [online] Available at: https://www.itma.ie/joyce [Accessed 2 Jun. 2018].

Jstor.org. (2018). Fairy Annals of Ulster. No. 2 on JSTOR. [online] Available at: http://www.jstor.org/stable/20563493?seq=1#page_scan_tab_contents [Accessed 17 Feb. 2018].

Jstor.org. (2018). On Methers and Other Ancient Drinking Vessels on JSTOR. [online] Available at: https://www.jstor.org/stable/25502588?seq=3#page_scan_tab_contents [Accessed 17 Feb. 2018].

Lashgoleor.ie. (2018). The Legend of Cú Chulainn, Lash Go Leor. [online] Available at: http://www.lashgoleor.ie/hurls_for_sale/cu_chulainn.html [Accessed 17 Feb. 2018].

Lasthunt.com. (2018). The Last Hunt. [online] Available at: http://lasthunt.com/hib1.html [Accessed 15 Feb. 2018].

Levysheetmusic.mse.jhu.edu. (2018). 099.041 - Temperance Song and Chorus. The Lips That Touch Liquor Shall Never Touch Mine. | Levy Music Collection. [online] Available at: http://levysheetmusic.mse.jhu.edu/collection/099/041 [Accessed 15 Feb. 2018].

Libraryireland.com. (2018). Fairy Archaeology and Medico-Religious Ceremonies. [online] Available at: http://www.libraryireland.com/IrelandSuperstitions/IV.php [Accessed 6 May 2018].

Libraryireland.com. (2018). Fosterage in Ancient Ireland. [online] Available at: http://www.libraryireland.com/Brehon-Laws/Fosterage.php [Accessed 6 May 2018].

Libraryireland.com. (2018). Irish Brigade at Fontenoy. [online] Available at: http://www.libraryireland.com/Atlas/LXXV-Irish-Brigade-Fontenoy.php [Accessed 6 May 2018].

Libraryireland.com. (2018). Irish Pipers in the Eighteenth Century. [online] Available at: http://www.libraryireland.com/IrishMusic/XXIII-2.php [Accessed 15 Feb. 2018].

Libraryireland.com. (2018). Walter Raleigh's House at Youghal, County Cork. [online] Available at: http://www.libraryireland.com/articles/RaleighYoughalDPJ1-48/ [Accessed 15 Feb. 2018].

Lyons, D. (2018). The Sprig of Shillelagh. [online] From-Ireland.net. Available at: http://www.from-ireland.net/song/the-sprig-of-shillelagh/ [Accessed 26 Oct. 2015].

Mabinogi.net. (2018). Cite a Website - Cite This For Me. [online] Available at: http://www.mabinogi.net/sections/ch%204/The_Expulsion_of_the_Deisi.pdf [Accessed 15 Feb. 2018].

McKeown, T. (2018). The Hell-Fire Clubs. [online] Freemasonry.bcy.ca. Available at: http://freemasonry.bcy.ca/history/hellfire/hellfire.html [Accessed 15 Feb. 2018].

Military-prints.com. (2018). Rodneys Formidable Breaking the Line 1782 by Charles Dixon. - Military-Prints.com. [online] Available at: http://www.military-prints.com/military_print.php?ProdID=3885 [Accessed 15 Feb. 2018].

Mocleirigh.ie. (2018). The Story of the Annals of the Four Masters | Mícheál Ó Cléirigh School. [online] Available at: http://mocleirigh.ie/travel-to-rossnowlagh/the-annals-of-the-four-masters [Accessed 15 Feb. 2018].

Sacred-texts.com. (2018). The Fairy-Faith in Celtic Countries: The Recorded Fairy-Faith: Chapter IV. People of the Goddess Dana. [online] Available at: http://www.sacred-texts.com/neu/celt/ffcc/ffcc240.htm [Accessed 6 May 2018].

Scarteen.net. (2018). Scarteen, Limerick, Ireland - Equestrian Venue, Event Horses, Hunting | Scarteen. [online] Available at: http://www.scarteen.net/ [Accessed 15 Feb. 2018].

Skinnerwallpaper.com. (2018). November | 2015 | David Skinner. [online] Available at: http://skinnerwallpaper.com/wordpress/?m=201511 [Accessed 15 Feb. 2018].

Snap.waterfordcoco.ie. (2018). Cite a Website - Cite This For Me. [online] Available at: http://snap.waterfordcoco.ie/collections/ebooks/106325/106325.pdf [Accessed 15 Feb. 2018].

The Irish Times. (2018). A rake's progress: Blazing Star: The Life & Times of John Wilmot. [online] Available at: https://www.irishtimes.com/culture/books/a-rake-s-progress-blazing-star-the-life-times-of-john-wilmot-1.1874726 [Accessed 15 Feb. 2018].

The Irish Times. (2018). New finds highlight Knockma's 'sacredlandscape'. [online] Available at: https://www.irishtimes.com/news/new-finds-highlight-knockma-s-sacred-landscape-1.1208951 [Accessed 6 May 2018].

The Irish Times. (2018). Rake's progress – An Irishman's Diary on the life, loves and wagers of Thomas 'Buck' Whaley. [online] Available at: https://www.irishtimes.com/opinion/rake-s-progress-an-irishman-s-diary-on-the-life-loves-and-wagers-of-thomas-buck-whaley-1.2902967 [Accessed 15 Feb. 2018].

thesession.org. (2018). The Session. [online] Available at: http://thesession.org/ [Accessed 2 Jun. 2018].

Tunearch.org. (2018). TTA - The Traditional Tune Archive. [online] Available at: http://tunearch.org/ [Accessed 2 Jun. 2018].

User, S. (2018). Home. [online] Irishdancingorg.com. Available at: http://www.irishdancingorg.com/web/ [Accessed 2 Jun. 2018].

We hope you enjoyed

JIGS to JACOBITES

The accompanying website

www.trad.dance

provides more information and a

JIGS to JACOBITES online shop.

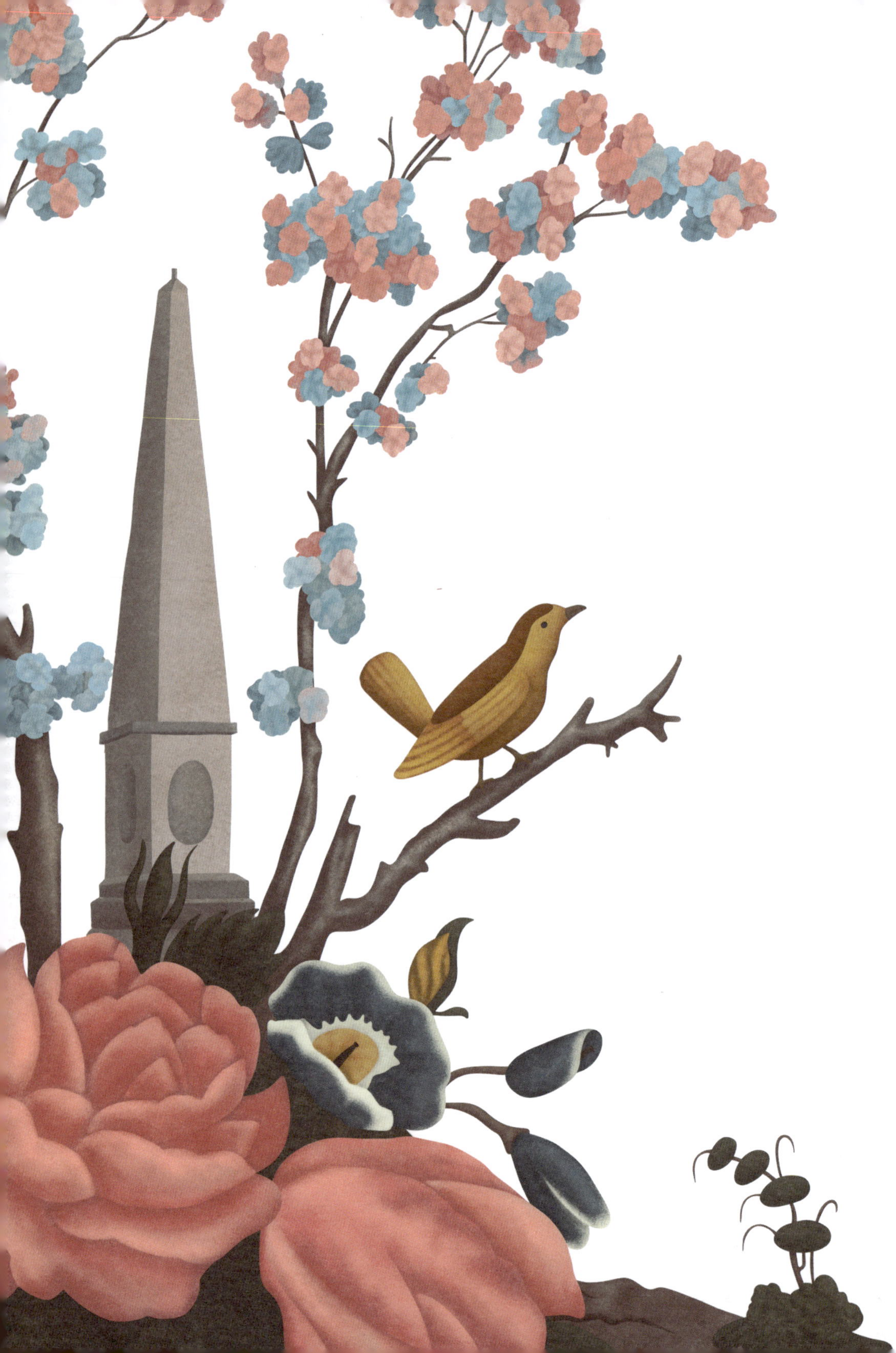